KIDNAPPED AT SIX

KIDNAPPED AT SIX

BASED ON REAL EVENTS

Pocket Full of Dreams

LORRAINE THERESA AUSTIN

XULON PRESS

Xulon Press
2301 Lucien Way #415
Maitland, FL 32751
407.339.4217
www.xulonpress.com

Paperback ISBN-13: 978-1-6628-1032-9
Ebook ISBN-13: 978-1-6628-1033-6

DEDICATION

For my one and only son, God's wonderful and precious gift to me. As my initial reviewer and editor, you lived my experience through my writing, as painful as it was for you. Without your encouragement to share my experience with the world, I would not have had the courage to write this book. My heart bursts with love and pride for you.

For my late parents, who loved their children unconditionally and sacrificed endlessly to give them a better life than the one they had. Their legacy of love for the Lord, their kindness, generosity, and genuine need to serve those less fortunate than themselves are blessings that I continue to cherish to this day. They laid the solid foundation for their children and the future generations to build on.

For my sisters, some of whom have to relive memories best forgotten, my sincere appreciation to all of you. Thank you so much for the therapeutic and restorative conversations that helped me find personal healing.

For my brothers, who supported my efforts to write this book. Thank you for always being my pillars of support. You continue to be our ever-ready warriors, who will do everything humanly and spiritually possible to defend and protect your sisters and all who are fortunate to be part of our extended family.

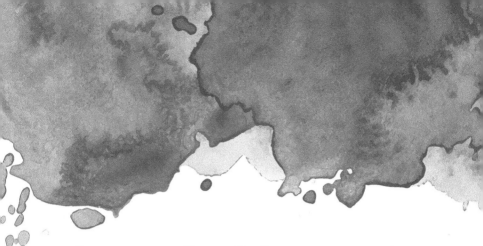

TABLE OF CONTENTS

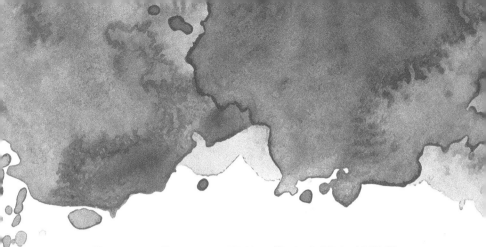

ACKNOWLEDGMENTS

SPECIAL THANKS TO my remarkable and amazing son for reviewing and editing my initial draft. Your guidance on website searches related to copyright compliance, assistance in obtaining free stock pictures, and ensuring they met the required standards for this book is priceless. Your time, patience and encouragement were integral in keeping me focused and on track for the successful completion of this book. You are my pride and joy.

Words are not enough to thank my charming and beautiful six-year-old niece for her good-natured and enthusiastic modeling in the rain, for my book cover. I will cherish forever her cheerful, lovely, and engaging smiles. Of course, capturing these pictures would not have been possible without her mother, who patiently photographed this beautiful child in the woods, in the rain! I am forever grateful to both of you.

Always thankful for my sisters and brothers and for their input about our early childhood and family life. Traveling down memory lane with all of you was a joyful exercise which I will cherish always.

I sincerely appreciate the assistance, expertise, and support I received from all representatives of Salem Author Services and Xulon Press. From my initial contact with Peter Lopez, Publishing Consultant, to my follow-up with Danielle Serta, Pre-Production Representative, and various other representatives from initial reviewer to editors, I was impressed at how much at ease they made me feel as I embarked on my very first attempt at writing.

Map of India

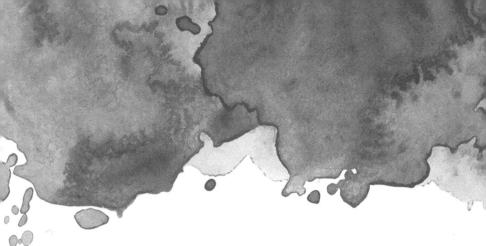

PREFACE

THE AUTHOR IS an Anglo-Indian (British-Indian) who grew up in a British colony town in the south of India. She was thrilled to immigrate to the USA as a young adult and became a US citizen as soon as it was possible to be sworn in. She is honored to identify herself as an Anglo-Indian-American. She is married to a natural-born American citizen of Scottish descent and lives in the USA. Her only child, an adult son, is her pride and joy.

Growing up Anglo-Indian had its advantages and disadvantages. Straddling two cultures can be a bit dodgy. Her British side with its open, carefree, fun-loving, whimsical celebration of life, filled with ballroom dancing, jam sessions, and musical talents, somehow had to blend in with her colorful Indian side with its rich traditions and diversity of customs, religions, and languages. Some have referred to the Anglo-Indians as an exotic cocktail, a mix of wonderful flavors that make up a deliciously potent and intoxicating drink. Others considered them as half-breeds, not accepted by the British nor by the Indians. She recalls preference was always given to scheduled cast and scheduled tribe in India, resulting in many Anglo-Indians (her parents included) incessantly searching for ways to immigrate to other countries, to make better lives for themselves and their children. Her parents prayed for an opportunity to leave India, to immigrate to a country that would offer their children an opportunity to improve their lives and a chance to excel in everything they put their minds to. Most of all, they longed for and dreamed about the day when their children would no longer be treated as second-class citizens.

British soldiers and gentlemen on assignment to India fell in love with the strikingly beautiful Indian women and set about charming them into marriage. The red/blond hair and blue eyes of the British gents, mixed with the gorgeous black hair and silky brown skin of the Indian ladies, made for stunningly beautiful children. However, after India's Independence from the British, most of the Britishers returned to their home country, some leaving behind their wives and children. A majority of these left-behind families in the author's hometown, though poor to middle class, carried themselves with great pride and dignity.

Life in her town was simple yet rewarding, filled with love, companionship, and people relying on each other for support. Family and community were the cornerstones of life. She loved her large, rowdy and rambunctious immediate and extended families.

However, her happy childhood was overshadowed by a truly traumatic event when she was very young. As a young adult, she promised herself she would face her demons one day and would find the courage to tell her story. But time passed and the ordeal remained stubbornly locked away in her subconscious, never to be tampered with. Fear of breaking the dam and opening herself up to the pain again prevented her from reaching into the furthermost recesses of her mind. Those memories were best left alone, locked away securely and never to be exposed. And, anyway, who would believe her after all these years?

Life moved on, she got married, immigrated to the USA, went through a difficult, abusive marriage which ended in divorce 18 months later. She became a US citizen within five years after entering the country and remarried. She helped all of her family members to immigrate too. Life in the USA provided innumerable opportunities for all of them and they were thrilled to have the entire family reunited and living in the same state with only a matter of a few miles separating them. America offered them the opportunities to complete college, build successful careers, businesses, marry and raise beautiful, talented children. They were blessed to have large extended families and a closeness that brought them together for weekly family dinners, every holiday, birthday, anniversary and every conceivable celebration. They cherished spending time together in their parents' home, sharing meals, playing various outdoor games and telling their children and grandchildren familiar old stories and ghost stories from back home. It was a wonderful way of building on traditions and memories for their children and grandchildren to follow as they eventually moved on to build their own lives and families. They loved America and living in America was a massive improvement compared to India. The heavenly father, America and life were certainly good to every one of them.

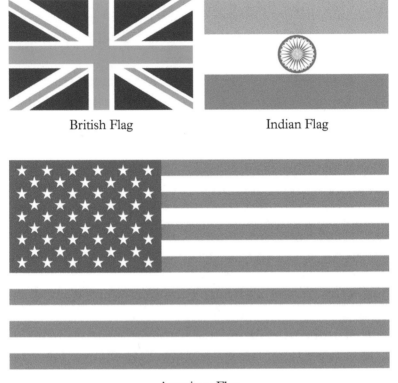

British Flag   Indian Flag

American Flag

Anglo-Indian-American

But then, the Coronavirus pandemic slammed the world with such brutal force that almost everything came to a standstill as friends and family were beat down by Covid-19 (including herself and several siblings and their families). Unemployment, lockdown, mask wearing, social distancing and all manner of restrictions became the new way of life. One can be forgiven for thinking straddling two cultures was the most difficult hurdle her family had to overcome, until Covid-19, the US election, and months of political commentary, negative advertisements, and civil unrest were piled on top. Straddling two political parties (Republicans and Democrats) within the family had the culture hurdle beat, hands down. But all was not lost, because with time on her hands, the author set about planning "social distancing" visits with her family members to stay connected and close, and she began to enjoy a renewed closeness with her siblings that had been pushed to the back burners when life was so hectic and busy.

One day while visiting with her nephew and his family, she had a revelation. She watched his six-year-old daughter sail down the staircase into the family room, as if she was walking on clouds. She was resplendent in her princess gown of pinks and purples, a tiara on her head, and a flowing, swinging cloak floating behind her petite little body. The author felt her chest tighten painfully as her heart stopped beating for a moment at the sight of this innocent and precious little girl, regally walking down the staircase, without a care in the world except to look like and act like a princess. Her eyes filled with tears as emotions got the better of her. The innocence, the purity, and the charm of this beautiful girl with her engaging smile and sparkling eyes filled her vision. Then forceful realization hit her. Her head began to spin and her vision blurred in reaction to the onslaught of emotions that crowded her mind and tightened like a vise around her heart. Oh God, she was exactly this age and as delicate in stature as this precious little girl, when her life was changed forever by a stranger. She must warn people or at least put them on alert about how quickly and easily a little girl's life could change and her joy stolen. One moment the child had no cares in the world, and within minutes her whole world could come crashing down around her.

This was reason enough to convince the author it was time to put into words what her mind had kept concealed.

All the fear and worry she had carried within her about being judged, or worse yet, not being believed, had to be squashed deliberately and replaced with hard-to-find courage to put pen to paper and start writing, start reliving those dreadful memories. She had to set aside the fear she had held on to for so long, like body armor or a shield, to keep people from learning about her secret. Those chains that bound her mind and soul had to be broken if she was to have any peace in her life

She must tell her story now. No more delays and no more excuses.

PROLOGUE

She was no older than six years of age, disoriented and experiencing moments of memory loss, but her exhausted brain compelled her to keep moving. Her captor could stumble upon her at any moment and at that thought, fear triggered another bout of panic, pushing her into motion.

Trudging forward on her tiny, tired, bare feet, her determination to escape him and find her way home was the only weapon she had to fight her fear of him and to keep her from drowning or fading away into the oblivion of the torrential downpour of the monsoon rains.

Rain

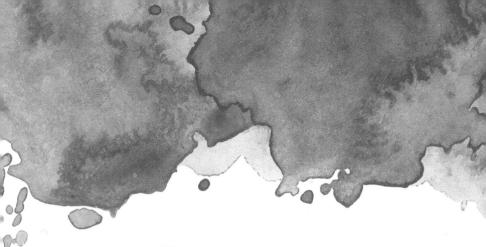

Chapter 1

LOST IN THE MONSOON

*God only gives you a storm because He knows you can handle
it. Rest assured, He will not allow you to suffer more than you
can endure. He will equip you with His strength. He will hold
your hand when you are too scared to take the next step. He will
carry you when you are at your weakest. In your darkest, bleakest
moments He will not abandon you.*

SHE WAS IN a strange place. It was almost, but not quite
pitch black. She couldn't see her hands in front of her. Her
teeth were chattering, her black hair was glued to her head
and face. She felt a chill in her bones like nothing she had
ever experienced before in her young life. Her child's brain
had no idea what to do, which direction to take, or how to
find shelter from the beating she was taking from the torrential downpour of monsoon rains. The rains had started earlier that afternoon and continued into the evening and night.

Countless questions kept popping into her head. Would
this rain ever stop? Would she drown in this unknown world
of darkness and unending deluge of water? Would her daddy

and mummy ever find her? Did they even know where to look for her? How would they know where this place was? In her head she screamed, *"Where am I? Am I in hell because I disobeyed my daddy and mummy?"* She panicked at the idea of hell, and all it stood for–the devil, the burning flames, and the sinners who didn't repent of their sins who were sent there to burn. And then she thought, *"Hell is supposed to have scorching fire, not rain!"* So, if she wasn't in hell, where was she? The fear that gripped her was so intense her chest hurt. She felt like she was suffocating. The darkness was beginning to settle around her like a thick, black mask over her head and shoulders. She was trapped in this place. Was this limbo? She knew when a person died there were three places they could go to. One was heaven, where Jesus lived, the other was hell where the devil lived, and the third place was called limbo. She didn't know much about limbo. She had not heard much about it except that it was a place where you were sent to wait until God decided where you belonged, heaven or hell. Maybe this was limbo!

Subconsciously, it registered in her brain that the rubber slippers she had been wearing earlier that day had long since been demolished by the rushing, churning, muddy waters that had steadily climbed until they reached her calves, and she was trudging through the muck barefoot. She was a petite, skinny six-year-old child. Each time the howling wind blew in her direction it pushed her backwards or sideways a couple steps. How long had she been wandering in this torturous place, the slush squishing between her toes together with the grass, wheat, or rice plants that had been beaten down by the heavy rains?

Occasionally she would feel something heavy and solid knock against her legs with a heavy thud, almost knocking her over, and then it would move away with the flowing and ebbing of the waters around her. Luckily, she didn't know and couldn't see whether it was a snake or small animal caught in the rains just like she was. God kept her from seeing such things in the rain that would have terrified her. Thank goodness she didn't know enough at that age to worry about snakes and other creepy-crawlies that infested those drenched rice or paddy fields. Her little heart wouldn't have been able to survive that thought. After all, at the age of six, her fear of snakes didn't stem from the thought of being bit but from the fact that the snake was representative of the devil. Thank God for small mercies.

She had lost all concept of time in the darkness. It seemed like days had passed since she had been playing with her siblings and neighborhood children on the pavement, in front of her home. What were they doing now at home? Were they all crying for her, were they scared for her, or were they angry with her? She feared her siblings might be angry with her, if they were punished and not allowed to play outside, because she went missing. Their parents had taught them to never talk to strangers, let alone go anywhere with them. But the man who took her wasn't a stranger, was he? He had been staying at her home for the past two or three days. Her uncle had brought him to visit from Bombay and her parents and other grown-ups were friendly with him. But her conscience pricked her. She should never have let him give her a ride on his bicycle. If they knew what he had been up to, she could just picture her dad and her uncles beating the living daylights out of him. In fact, she wished they would catch him and beat him up so he was as scared as she was. He needed to be punished. Maybe he should be sent to hell for what he had done.

Hunger pangs gnawed at her stomach. It was so empty she thought her stomach was touching her backbone because it had shriveled up with hunger. She opened her mouth and swallowed huge gulps of rainwater. It made her cough uncontrollably as she choked on it. But no one would hear her in this desolate place. She couldn't see a thing in front of her or around her. Thunder boomed and brilliant lightening lit up the sky sporadically. Even though the sound of the thunder startled and scared her out of her mind every time it resounded across her darkened world, she was thankful for the lightening that followed and illuminated the space surrounding her. However, her hopes were dashed and she was disappointed, because each time all it revealed was emptiness. There were no roads, no buildings, no people or animals to suggest there was life, or hope. Hope! That was not a word she understood at all, but it definitely was a feeling she sensed deep inside her. She couldn't have described this feeling if asked to.

Lightning

Fear and panic gripped her again and again as she let her thoughts wander to the possibilities of never getting back home, never seeing her family again, never experiencing again her mummy's hand feeding her mouthfuls of rice and curry from the community pot from which her sisters and brothers were being fed. Her heart pounded loud in her chest and in her ears and this new experience scared her. Years later, she would understand the pounding she felt in her chest and ears was pure panic.

Was her childish innocence her saving grace? Did it keep her from going crazy because she didn't really know the dangers out there in the darkness? Or did a superior power keep her from that knowledge that would have destroyed her mind? She didn't know it then, but yes, of course, it was the Almighty God, the Good Shepherd who leaves the ninety-nine sheep behind to find that one lost one. And was she ever lost! He was the force right there beside her, guiding her, helping her place one bare foot in front of the other, without faltering, without falling, keeping her awake, keeping her alive, keeping her from losing her mind, leading her.

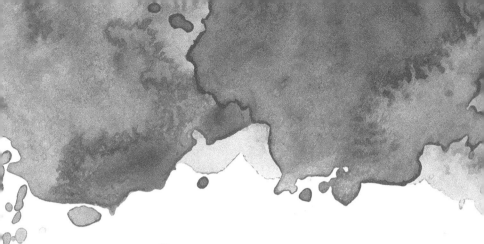

CHAPTER 2

FINDING HER SANCTUARY IN PRAYER

"You will seek me and find me, when you seek me with all your heart." Jeremiah 29:13

SHE DIDN'T WANT to think about what had transpired earlier that day, but hours of wandering, and the unrelenting downpouring of those legendary monsoon rains couldn't prevent the thoughts of that horrible man from snaking back into her mind. It left her feeling scared and apprehensive, afraid he might find her and do unthinkable things to her again. She suffered another panic attack at the thought of him, and her stomach tightened into painful knots as bile filled her throat and mouth and burned along her nostrils. She could not control her bodily reaction and she vomited the bitter bile that had filled her mouth. Her stomach continued to heave for several moments, though there was nothing left for her to throw up. It was an uncomfortable and painful reaction to her thoughts of him, so she tried to force herself to think of something else.

Thank God he didn't have her captive anymore. She would much rather be lost and in this scary place than with that monster of a man. He was definitely more frightening to her than the hard, cold monsoon rains. But wait, what if he found her? Panic again! She couldn't tell if he had followed her because it was so black around her. But, as quickly as that thought crossed her mind, her Heavenly Father most decisively steered her away from the memory of what had transpired earlier that evening with that wicked beast of a man, by channeling her thoughts in a different direction, the direction of survival and rescue.

She knew she should pray but she didn't know how to pray, what words to use, for the situation she was in. Maybe she could just repeat the prayers she had learned with her siblings in Catholic church. Yes, she knew three or four prayers by heart, the "Our Father," the "Hail Mary" and the "Glory Be," and her night prayer, and she half-remembered others. Would God understand she was saying these prayers in hopes He would help her find her way back home? And not allow that man to find her? At the thought of him, she went into another fit of panic and with a trembling voice, she recited those prayers she remembered, over and over again.

Our Father, who art in heaven
Hallowed be thy name,
Thy kingdom come,
Thy will be done
On earth, as it is in heaven
Give us this day our daily bread,

Forgive us our trespasses
As we forgive those who trespass against us,
And lead us not into temptation
But deliver us from evil. Amen.
(Matthew 6:9-13 NRSV & Luke 11:2-4 NRSV

***Hail Mary**, full of grace*
The Lord is with thee,
Blessed art thou amongst women
And blessed is the fruit of thy womb, Jesus.
Holy Mary, mother of God
Pray for us sinners
Now and at the hour of our death. Amen.
(Traditional Catholic Prayer)

***Glory Be** to the Father,*
And to the Son,
And to the Holy Spirit,
As it was in the beginning
Is now and ever shall be
World without end. Amen.
(Traditional Catholic Prayer)

She lost count of how many times she recited these prayers. Hundreds, maybe thousands of times she repeated them, over and over again. She recited them out loud, and each time she repeated them she tried to imagine what each sentence in those prayers really meant. She pictured God the Father seated on His golden throne in heaven until He seemed so real to her, as if He was right in front of her. She pictured Jesus also on a throne seated next to God, wearing beautiful garments of whites and blues. In her mind, it was the most beautiful, breathtaking sight she had ever seen. She thought she must already have been transported to heaven as she repeated her prayers. Yet, she was afraid to reach out and touch Jesus' or His Father's beautiful clothes.

She pictured Mary, the mother of Jesus, who was at first frightened by the angel that appeared in front of her, and then she imagined Mary holding the baby Jesus and smiling down at Him. She wanted to pinch the baby Jesus' cheeks just like all the visitors who pinched her cheeks when they visited, which signaled that they thought she was cute.

In her mind's eye she saw the angels, larger than life itself, as they surrounded Jesus and God the Father, in their long, flowing, snowy white gowns and soft white feathered wings, with golden halos around their heads. They looked exactly like the tall statutes at Sacred Heart Church where she went to Mass on some Sundays, and on special occasions like Christmas and Easter, except that they were real.

She thought about how special she felt when she was in church. The smell of the jasmine garlands hanging around the necks of the statutes of Jesus and Mother Mary at the altar and the saints around the church, combined with the smell of the hundreds of burning candles and the aromatic smoke from the incense burners, which always made her feel so relaxed and calm. She loved to hear the church congregation reciting the prayers, the choir singing, the pipe organ resounding and echoing through the high ceilings throughout the church. And most of all, she impatiently waited to hear the church bells ring out loud from the belfry (bell tower) so she could feel the melodious sounds vibrating resoundingly through her small body. She couldn't explain it, but she could feel the sound of those bells deep in her being as her blood carried it to every fiber of her body. It was the most exhilarating feeling she experienced in her young life, and even as an adult she became nostalgic when she heard church bells ring. She would love to linger there in the church and let her imagination transport her to places she had never been. She wanted to spend time in this quiet, pleasant daydream.

Jasmine Flowers

She was so engrossed in the prayers, her imagination of heaven and Jesus, and the memories of her church visits, she forgot her worries and fears for a little while during those hours of wandering and praying in the darkness. How wonderful it was that a child could forget the outside world and reside in her daydreams where magic and fun took center stage and the rest of the world just faded away into oblivion.

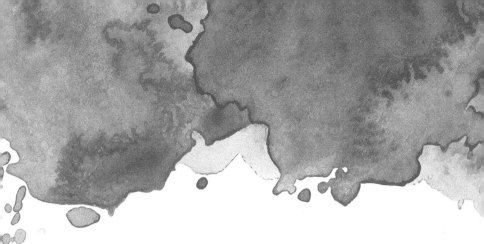

Chapter 3

Visions of a Six-Year-Old

RATHER THAN ALLOW her to return to the reality of her predicament, her wandering mind intentionally visualized heaven instead. She imagined it being so beautiful, with lovely gardens that stretched on forever and ever. Astonishingly, she could actually smell the flowers as if they were growing along the pathway in the rain. In her mind she could identify the mayflower trees, jasmine, marigold, and queen of the night flowers. She inhaled deeply to trap their perfume in her memory forever. She could see birds fluttering around, chirping and singing sweetly as they sailed on the air from one flowering tree to another. She even pictured fruit trees, like mango, guava, jackfruit, pomegranate, butterfruit (avocado), custard apple, wood apple, bullsheart, papaya, cashapple, gooseberries, and mulberries, some of which she enjoyed from their own compound at home, and others when her father could afford to purchase such luxuries for a special treat for them. She closed her eyes so she could savor the memory of their sweet/tart deliciousness on her tastebuds. She longed to be back home in her compound with her siblings. She could picture them climbing up the guava tree (though she couldn't climb very high), hanging on to the branches, plucking the fruit even before they were ripe enough to eat. She also remembered watching the fruit vendors park their bandy-carts near the bus stop in from of her home and hoping that her parents or uncles would buy her and the other children sugarcane juice, tender coconuts or ice-apples to quench their thirst on blistering hot summer days.

Bullsheart Tree

Custard Apple Tree

Coconut Tree

Jackfruit Tree

CashApple Tree (Cashew Nut)

Papaya Fruit

Guava Tree

But alongside these happy thoughts of her home and family, a feeling of loss and sadness infiltrated her mind and spread through her veins, carrying those heavy feelings to her entire body. She endeavored to steer away from the sad feelings, which provoked piercing pains behind her eyelids and in the deepest parts of her heart, and concentrate on her vision of Heaven again.

Back to her daydream, she pictured butterflies and drag-onflies floating around in the air, their colors so vibrant she couldn't stop staring at them. The colorful yet transparent wings of the dragonfly fascinated her. One day she would be able to catch a dragonfly of her own and she would give it a special name. She wished she could turn into a butterfly or a bird and fly back home. But once she got back home, she would somehow turn back into being herself again.

Butterflies

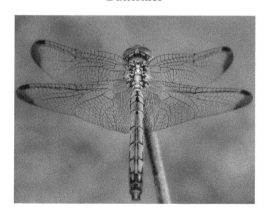

Dragonflies

There were definitely no mud roads in heaven like there was in her hometown. She saw the smoothest roads made of marble and see-through glass, not like the busy, crowded streets she was used to, where autorickshaws, scooters, bicycles, bullock-carts, cows, goats, dogs and people competed for their own piece of the road. She could hear drivers yelling out, horns honking or blaring, brakes screeching, cows mooing and goats bleating, in the noisy commotion and splendor of her Main Street. Noise didn't bother her, though, as she was used to being awakened at 4 am by the chanting of the temple prayers over the loud-speaker from across the street, followed by the singing from the mosque behind her home, also over the loud-speaker, or the ear-splitting sound of the factory siren.

Bullock Cart

Bullock Cart

Horse and Carriage

Traffic

Traffic

Autorickshaw

Street Life

The roads in heaven were so blissfully quiet with only soft, soothing music floating on the gently scented air. She could skip and dance to her heart's content along heaven's roads without fear or the danger of being hit by a vehicle or knocked over by an animal. There was definitely no chance of her stepping into fresh, warm dung on the sidewalk. This place was immaculately clean. She loved heaven and wouldn't mind staying forever, so long as she could have her family with her.

There were rainbows arching across the heavens in brilliant hues with soft, fluffy white clouds drifting gently along. The grass was so green and luxuriously soft, she could easily lie down and fall into a dreamy sleep where her whole world would be right again. She could even roll down the hill and not get hurt, or watch her dad and uncles fly a kite in these wide, open spaces of heaven.

Rainbow

The whole of heaven was like a magic garden that stretched on and on, with something more spectacular to see around each bend or turn in the landscape. She followed a smooth pebble stone walkway and noticed vines curling around white fencing and beautiful, brilliantly colored flowers turning their faces to the sun. Softly curved white benches were tucked into little nooks everywhere for passersby to sit and rest their feet on the lush green moss, which felt as soft and smooth as silk between her toes. Rounded bushes with larger-than-life flowers surrounded the pathway. A closer look into the bushes revealed birds, butterflies and other insects she couldn't name, hovering over the flowers, wings fluttering softly as they sipped at their nectar.

In the distance, the gentle swaying of palm trees and other flowering trees caught her eye and beckoned her to investigate. She imagined she saw a white swing hanging from one of those trees with yellow flowers twining their way up the ropes of the swing. If she squinted hard enough, she could see fairies pushing a little girl who looked just like her on the swing, high up into the sky. She felt exhilarated because she had never sat on a swing before. One day she would learn to swing like that little girl and she would float high up in the sky and see the whole world. The thought filled her with happiness and longing.

Peaceful Meadow

Flower Gardens

Garden Bridge

Garden Bench

Playground Swing

As she continued along the picturesque walkway, she heard the sound of laughter and she quickly moved toward the happy sound. She came to a clearing and stopped to gaze in amazement at little boys and girls around her age, playing games she recognized. Some of the children were riding bicycles, some children were riding on painted horses, camels, lions, and tigers on a Merry-Go-Round, and others were playing a familiar playground game she loved.

She stopped excitedly to watch them play. They stood in a circle while the leader wove in and out between each child in a zigzag pattern as they sang the first verse.

"In and out the sparkling bluebells,
In and out the sparkling bluebells,
In and out the sparkling bluebells,
I am the leader."

The leader stopped behind a child at the end of the first verse. When they began singing the chorus, the leader tapped both her palms on the child's shoulders while the children sang:

"Rap-a-tap-a-tap-tap on my shoulder,
Rap-a-tap-a-tap-tap on my shoulder,
Rap-a-tap-a-tap-tap on my shoulder,
I am the leader."

Then the new child became the leader, and the previous leader, keeping her hands on the new leader's shoulders, followed her as she wove her way in and out of the circle of children, repeating this song until all the children had an opportunity to become the leader.

Her heart longed to join in as she remembered how much fun she and her siblings had with the neighbor children when they played these playground games. But there was so much more to see. The children were so happy here. They had so many lovely toys and games to play. And there were many, many angels everywhere, with their wide, feathery wings floating around them in slow motion, stopping every now and then to hug a child or whisper something in their ears and point to something in the distance.

When her legs grew heavy and weary, she sat down on a stone bench and looked around her curiously, taking in the sights and sounds, trying to store up mental pictures of everything for future reference and enjoyment. Wait a minute! Wasn't that the duck pond from the park behind her house? It looked just like it, with its stone pillars and surrounding walls and flowers. There were flowers growing all around the pond and the ducks were swimming back and forth, dipping their heads into the water. As they raised their heads and shook the water off, the droplets cascaded downward like a waterfall of diamonds as they caught the sun. It was such a beautiful sight that it took her breath away.

She was dead tired, but she tried to keep her eyes open to take in more of the pleasing surroundings. She wanted to remember this place and tried to memorize every last detail so she could tell her parents and her siblings when she got back home. Her eyelids grew heavier with each passing second until fatigue took over, and she dozed off peacefully in this happy place.

All was quiet as she slept the sleep of the innocence. There was a hush over all of heaven, as if God had commanded that everyone be quiet while she slept. And then, into her dreams, softly and quietly penetrated a vision of an indiscernible being settling onto the bench beside her, gently touching her shoulders and back, and a tender voice calling her name quietly, saying "Time to wake up and keep moving, my child."

She woke up slowly, rubbing her eyes with a deep sigh. She wondered if that was God who had just spoken to her. It had been so calm and peaceful in her dreams. Had He heard her prayers and was speaking to her now? Could He really tell it was her? How did her prayers reach Him, so far up above the skies, especially with the loud thunder she could still hear resounding around her? Did they float up to Him in heaven in her voice or did they magically get written across the sky for Him to read? She wished someone was there to explain this to her.

But reality set in as she slowly became aware that she must have just awakened out of a lovely dream, because she was still walking, putting one foot in front of the other, like a robot, without thinking about it. She could hear and feel the rains beating down hard on her body and it was still dark all around her. How long had she been walking in this dark world? She had no idea if she had been walking forward or whether she had turned around and walked back in the direction she had come from. Maybe she had been walking in circles and had made no progress at all. It was so dark! She would just have to keep praying even louder to make sure God heard her, and maybe He would send one of His angels to rescue her. Maybe the angel could carry her so she could rest her aching legs. If she asked nicely, would the angel be able to give her a cardigan so she could feel warm again? She longed to be transported back to that place in her mind again so she could escape this dreadful reality. But try as she might, she could not will her mind to return to that place. The connection was broken, at least for the moment.

CHAPTER 4

THE HOLY SPIRIT COMFORTS HER

He that dwelleth in the secret place of the Most High shall abide
under the shadow of the Almighty. I will say of the Lord, "He is
my refuge and my fortress, my God, in whom I trust." Surely he
will save you from the fowler's snare and from the deadly pestilence.
Psalm 91:1

WERE HER VISIONS of God and heaven, the angels and Jesus, the sights and the sounds just her imagination? Was her mind creating these visions as a form of self-protection against the real world she was traveling through? Was it survival instinct? Or, on the other hand, had she been transported to heaven for real? Was her experience real or in her mind? Was she actually walking through heaven and experiencing it in her dream-like state? She just knew she was there and she had experienced a world of such amazing wonder and beauty that she had never experienced before. Heaven or not, she didn't want to leave this place, this sanctuary. And, if she had to leave, she didn't want to forget it. She wished her parents and siblings could see it, too. They would love it so much and they would thank her for finding it.

She had no idea that her fervent and persistent praying was really an outpouring of faith in a God she could not see in the dark world she was wandering through. She knew instinctively if she prayed hard enough, He would hear her and He would help her. She didn't know it, but this God whom she had never seen or met before knew the childlike purity and sincerity of her heart, even though she didn't quite know what those prayers meant as she recited them a thousand times over in those long, lost hours.

She didn't know she had reached this Almighty God, and He was about to perform a miracle in her young, innocent life that had been turned upside down, and it would last her lifetime, sustaining her through many trials, heartaches and challenges in the future. She would learn soon enough that she would grow in faith because she knew Him as her Lord and Savior at a very tender age when she was lost and crying out for His help in the monsoon.

Yet, those were not lost hours after all. He came to her rescue in a quiet, unthreatening, unassuming way. He led her to the light, literally. At that age, she only understood things in the literal sense. She was not old enough to understand miracles or the presence of the Holy Spirit or God Himself. She didn't understand the concept of the Holy Trinity. The understanding of the Holy Spirit's presence would come years later, together with visions or premonitions of potential danger. She would develop a keen instinctiveness or intuitiveness that steered her away from danger and saved the day on several occasions.

Did she choose to believe in a God she couldn't see because she was afraid and needed something or someone to cling to rather than her fear? Was this unseen God less scary than her fear? Or did He choose to save an innocent child from the perils of the nightmare world she found herself in so she would become His devoted advocate years down the road?

She felt a sense of peace, though she didn't know the meaning of that word. She clung to that feeling, hugging it to her shivering body. It seemed to calm her jumpy nerves. Somehow, she felt He was listening to her as she felt His presence around her. She didn't know how or why, but she knew He was there with her now, that He was the very air she was breathing.

She continued on through the night like a blind person in the darkness that surrounded her, placing one tired foot in front of the other, her pace slow and labored, not able to see the world around her. She wasn't even sure if the world existed anymore. Maybe she had stepped off the end of the world and she was in some place that had no people or animals, only rain and darkness. After all the blind wandering she had done, she no longer had any sense of direction. For the rest of her life, she would be challenged by a poor sense of direction, even with a map or GPS for guidance. As an adult, she lost count of the many times she had lost her way while driving!

As her mind settled into oblivion, she was unaware that she had unconsciously retreated into the sanctity of the sanctuary she had created in her mind. One would have to see through the eyes of a six-year-old to understand the bleakness she felt and her need for a special sanctuary to crawl into and hide. During her life, when the stormy clouds of life threatened, she would take shelter in her sanctuary. Though she was a fierce fighter and could hold her own in almost any situation, it was reassuring to know she could retreat to her sanctuary when the stress, fear, and emotions got the better of her. There was always a toasty, welcoming light in her sanctuary that warmed her chilled bones and gave her burdened heart the respite it desperately needed. It kept at bay the darkness and hopelessness that threatened to overcome her.

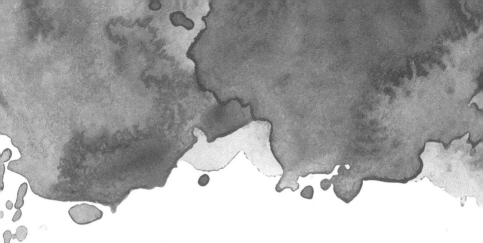

CHAPTER 5

THE VISITOR

"Do not forget to show hospitality to strangers, for by so doing
some people have shown hospitality to angels without knowing it."
Hebrews 13:2

THE GIRL'S UNCLE lived and worked in Bombay, India.
He mingled with actors, people from the film industry and
people from all walks of life. He was her mother's younger
brother, a jovial, fun-loving and trusting chap. He visited her
family in the south of India on several occasions during the
year, often bringing friends, people he'd run into or people
from the movie industry. Her father always welcomed her
mother's family members, who frequently stayed with them
for prolonged periods of time while transitioning from one
job to another.

Her parents were decent and respectable people. They
were courteous and generous hosts. Though they didn't
have much, they always shared meals and refreshments, or
whatever they had available at the time, with anyone in need,
and offered them a place to rest their heads for a night or

two. There was always a kettle on the stove for tea or coffee for visitors.

The house was a typical British colony bungalow-style home. It was a small house with a hall room (living room), a single bedroom, a veranda which separated the house from the kitchen, and an outhouse without a roof or a door. Her father eventually built a roof over it and added a door for privacy. There was a compound with lots of trees and plants. Most of the homes on this side of town were owned or rented by the descendants of British men who had married Indian women or British-Indian women and settled in India.

Anglo-Indians spoke excellent English, had a British education and dressed like Britishers. Though not well off by any means, most Anglo-Indian households engaged a servant or two to help with household chores and assistance with the children in exchange for meals and a small pay, and sometimes a small corner of the compound for sleeping arrangements if the servant needed a place to live.

Her parents, the womenfolk and the children slept on beds, cots or on straw mats on the floor inside the house. The climate was hot and more often than not the windows and doors were left wide open to encourage summer breezes to drift through the house. The men (mostly uncles on her mother's side) together with any male visitors were relegated to the compound to sleep on bedsheets or straw mats on the ground. They didn't mind these outdoor sleeping arrangements under the shelter of the guava and other fruit trees. They relished the idea of gazing at the twinkling stars through the swaying branches and leaves and enjoyed talking or telling tall tales late into the night until sleep finally claimed them.

On this particular trip, her uncle brought a friend along who was supposedly AWOL from the Indian military and was hiding out for a couple days in South India. He had no place to stay, so her parents, true to their generous nature, welcomed him and made him feel at home. Her parents never turned anyone away. They trusted people and extended their hospitality to anyone and everyone in need.

By day two of the Visitor's stay, everyone was comfortable around him and he was pretty much accepted as someone who could be trusted. He hung out with the adults, chatting, eating, and being entertained. The children didn't know much about him except that he seemed to be getting along well with the adults. They were not impressed with his military status, primarily because they didn't know much about the military and hardly ever saw a military person in their town.

At some point on the second evening, the Visitor ventured outdoors and started chatting with the children. He showed off the bicycle he had rented for the day. He offered to give each of the children a ride (riding "doubles") on his bicycle "just around the block and back." Everyone took turns to sit on the crossbar in front of him and he took each child around the block for a ride. This was a rare treat for the children. So, when he offered a second ride, they were thrilled and happy to take full advantage of another turn on the bike with him.

Then it was time for the girl to take her second ride with "the Visitor." She climbed up on the crossbar (side-saddle) as before and he started to pedal. When he got to the end of the block, instead of going around the bend, he kept going further up the street. She questioned why he was going up the street and he responded that he wanted to go a little further. When they got to the very top of the street ("up the road" as the children referred to it) and he turned the corner so that she couldn't see her family home anymore, she demanded that he take her back home, stating that her mummy and daddy would be angry with her if she went any further. But he told her he was just taking her for a longer ride than the others because she was special. She repeated she didn't want to go any further with him and he should take her back home because her parents would be angry with her. But, of course, he didn't listen to her because he had other intentions. Intentions that she was too young to understand or to even have some premonition about. All she knew was that her parents would be angry with her for leaving the safety and security of their neighborhood block. She couldn't understand why he would want to go so far away from her home, especially since it was getting darker and later.

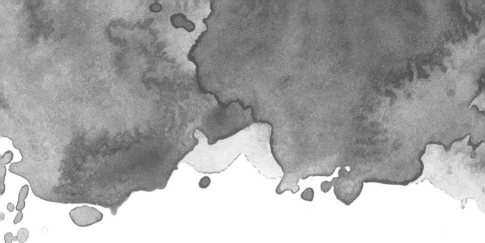

CHAPTER 6

KIDNAPPED IN PLAIN SIGHT

INSTEAD OF TURNING around, he pedaled faster and faster. She begged and pleaded for him to turn around and tried to slide off the crossbar, ignoring any fear of injuring herself or causing an accident. But she was imprisoned within the circle of his big, strong arms, which gripped the handlebar and held her to his chest. She was trapped and scared. She didn't like the feel of his body so close to hers, and she didn't like the way his face kept brushing against her head. She didn't understand the utter revulsion she felt every time any part of his body made contact with hers. She knew it felt wrong. The tiny hairs on the back of her neck and back stood on end, sending chills running down her spine. She shivered at this brand-new experience she couldn't understand, except that it made her feel sick deep down in her stomach. She learned in the future to pay attention to the sensation of the hair on the back of her neck and back sending chills down her spine because it was a warning or indication of potential, lurking danger. A sixth sense!

She cried and pleaded for him to turn back toward home, tears running down her cheeks, into her mouth and down the front of her neck, but he became irritated and angry with her, telling her to keep quiet and stop annoying him. And to add to her misery, it started to rain. In minutes they were both totally drenched. The rain got heavier, and the skies became darker by the minute as thunder rolled and rumbled, and lightning streaked across the dark skies. She was absolutely terrified. But still, the man kept pedaling, propelling them further into the darkness. She was trapped and afraid. She didn't know at that time that these were the notorious monsoon rains, which could go on for days, wreaking havoc on people and property, clogging up the already blocked drainage system, and causing heavy flooding.

The Lord only knew how long and how far they travelled. She knew it was way out of her hometown because they had passed her church, her school and everything she was familiar with. She couldn't tell how long they had been on the road, but to her it seemed like hours because it was way past her supper time by now and she was so hungry and tired. She didn't recognize any of the streets, the stores or buildings. The farther away they got, the less she recognized anything, and the more panicked she became.

On and on into the evening he cycled, refusing to listen to her pleas, getting angrier with her for crying, and threatening to slap her face if she didn't shut up. She continued to cry loudly and he resorted to pinching her arm really hard, or thumping her on her back and shoulders with his fist in anger. The pain from the blows did nothing to stem the flow of tears, barely registering in fact, because her fear was larger than life itself. Her crying eventually changed to deep, heart-wrenching sobs, but he was unmoved. He had only one goal in mind, to get to his destination, wherever that was. He was not going to let the rains stop him from attaining his goal. The nice friend of her uncle had morphed into a scary, fearful stranger.

Gradually she became aware of a new danger. She didn't understand it, but she sensed it. The first time he placed his big hand on her thigh, she almost jumped right out of her skin. She was terrified at his action and hit his hand off her thigh with such force that he almost toppled the bicycle. No one had ever done that to her before! What did he think he was doing? She didn't know why it made her feel so scared and so sick at the same time. She felt a shiver run down her spine and the fine hairs on the back of her neck stood up again, like before. She couldn't describe her feelings but whatever the feeling was, it was doing a slow, agonizing crawl from her head to her toes, making her feel like her body was being invaded by hundreds of ants or spiders. It was a feeling she had when she was scared during the telling of a ghost story by her uncles or neighbors. She knew that sensation meant she was scared about what was about to happen next.

The further they got, the bolder his hand became. A few minutes later he placed his hand on her thigh again over her skirt and began to move it up and down, getting closer to her knickers (panties). She cringed violently in disgust and revulsion, almost knocking them off the bike each time, as she tried to move on the crossbar to get away from his hand. She was so scared. But he was relentless in his attempts to touch her intimately. She was confused. What was he trying to do to her? No one had ever tried to do that to her before. Why would an adult person try to touch her there? She was shaken to her core by this new fear. If her mummy found out what he was doing, she would slipper-whack him across his face. That would serve him right. Her mummy was not afraid of any man. She would not hesitate to bend down and take her slipper off her foot and turn around and slap him really hard across his face with it. But, if her mummy told her daddy what this man was trying to do, her daddy would not use his slipper, he would hit him with his bare fists and would probably break all his bones. Of this she was certain.

After an eternity of her squirming and him trying his darndest to assault her on the bicycle, he started to slow down, searching for something. He peered into the darkness that had settled in. What was he looking for? What was he going to do? Would she be able to run away when he stopped the bike? Which way should she run? Questions kept popping into her head, but she didn't know the answers. She was so totally lost and helpless. She was trapped on this crossbar with his arms tightly surrounding her body as he gripped the handlebar. She wished her daddy and her uncles could find her soon. She just knew they could fight him and beat him up and then rescue her and take her back home.

What if she bit his arm really hard? Would she be able to jump off the bike and run? She thought she had the courage to try that. Her thoughts swirling around in her brain, like a cyclone, were dizzying. Her head was beginning to pound, like a hundred drums were being banged at the same time. What should she do? Her stomach began to churn uncomfortably. She felt so ill. Her brain could not come up with a plan no matter how hard she tried.

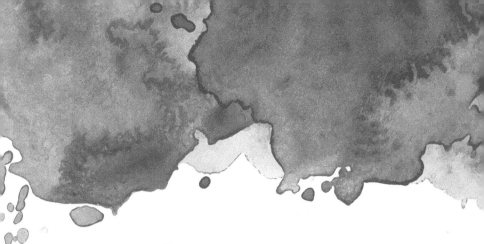

CHAPTER 7

THE HOTEL

You may be in the worst storm of your life, yet He knows exactly where you are. He is the all-knowing and all-seeing God, the Rock of Ages. He is the very air that you breathe.

THE GIRL WAS so caught up in her thoughts of escape that she hardly noticed they had reached some sort of town, until the man finally stopped and propped his bicycle against a wall, instructing her to wait beside it while he went inside a very, very tall building. As he moved away from her, she became aware again that the rains continued to pour down on her aching head and shoulders. The street was deserted with not a soul in sight. There was no shelter or awning to shelter her from the rain. She was too scared to move and dared not disobey his orders, so she waited patiently for his return. She needed to use the bathroom to vee-vee. They had not stopped anywhere to use the bathroom and she felt that her stomach would burst with the pressure she was feeling. She danced from leg to leg, trying to hold her bladder, but finally it became too much for her

41

and she felt the hot liquid run down her legs right where she was standing. She was glad that the rains immediately washed the urine away. No one would ever know since her clothes were wringing wet. Yet, she felt ashamed and guilty about this little mishap.

Standing there, rooted to the spot next to the bicycle, she had no thought to run away. Many years later when she questioned herself, she knew why she did she not have the presence of mind to make a dash for it, to just leave the bike there and run away. It was because, as young as she was, obedience had been drilled into her by her parents. She knew following instructions from adults was of paramount importance and his command to "stay here" literally kept her rooted to the spot.

After what seemed an eternity to her, he returned and informed her they were going inside the building to dry off and to get something to eat. He led her inside, with another stern warning to keep quiet. She realized many years later that they probably entered the hotel through the back entrance since there was no lobby or reception desk, just long, winding corridors of closed doors that seemed to go on for miles and miles. They made their way along the carpeted corridors quietly. By now she had stopped crying and looked around curiously at the massive building with humungous carved doors and high ceilings. She thought the dark wooden doors extended from the floor to the sky. She was so intimidated by the size of these doors, she stopped in her tracks, refusing to budge. Though she wondered what was behind those closed doors, she would not give in to her inquisitiveness and explore because of fear of what was actually there. She felt so tiny and insignificant next to them. What if one of them fell on her and crushed her? Her parents would never find her if that happened because she would be trapped under it. Squashed like a small bug under a huge shoe.

Or, what if some huge monsters or the boogieman were hiding behind those doors and were waiting for her to enter, to eat her up? Seeing her fear, the man became impatient with her. Grabbing her, he dragged her along the corridor until he reached the end of it and unlocked a door. He shoved her into the room and turned and locked the door. The sound of the lock turning was the most frightening sound she'd heard in her whole life. Why did he lock the door? They didn't have any locks on the doors in her home. She quickly tried to unlock the door to run out, but she couldn't reach the latching device, even standing on her tippy toes. He grabbed her away from the door and shoved her into the room. She almost lost her balance and fell, but caught herself just in time.

She straightened up as her mind registered the scene in front of her. She saw the room was so large and beautiful. Even in her fear, it took her breath away. She had never seen anything like it in her entire life. She didn't know what a fireplace looked like, had never even heard of such a thing, but there was one at the other end of the room, with a welcoming heat that penetrated the room and reached its warm tentacles across to her cold, shivering body and made her feel gloriously warm and welcome. Had she died and gone to heaven? The deeply cushioned sofa and the huge, high bed beckoned her exhausted body and she just wanted desperately to float over to the bed and curl up on the soft looking blankets and sleep for a very, very long time. If her daddy was here, she wouldn't have to walk, he would carry her tired body to the bed and cover her with a warm blanket to make her comfortable and safe.

But she was rudely awakened out of her dreamland state when he advanced toward her. Fear engulfed her. Sheer terror and panic set in at the thought of being locked in this room with him. What should she do? She was like a trapped animal at the mercy of a giant monster. Her eyes wide with fear, she looked around desperately for a way to escape him. Where could she run to? The windowsills were too high for her to even try to climb on to them to try to open the windows. The furniture looked very heavy, just like the expense box (wooden trunk with metal bolts and hinges) in their hall room at home, which held their rations for the month. She knew she would not be able to budge any of the chairs. There was nowhere she could hide in this room, no escape. She would have been less afraid of the floor opening up and swallowing her whole than she was facing off with this man.

She didn't know what to do, yet she kept looking for a way out of that room. She was transfixed with absolute fear and the dread that flowed through every fiber of her being and threatened to overpower her. But, even in her fear, she half-remembered warnings from her parents about staying clear of strangers. It was as clear as it could be to a six-year-old that rescue was not going to happen, she was at a dead end in this hotel room. She had to find her own way out. Survivor that she was, her mind would not tolerate defeat. She might have been small and afraid, but she was a fighter, and all of a sudden, the very fear that had engulfed her all through the ride gave way to a fierce will to fight. It sparked her determination to fight him with all her might. He had no idea what he had unleashed in her!

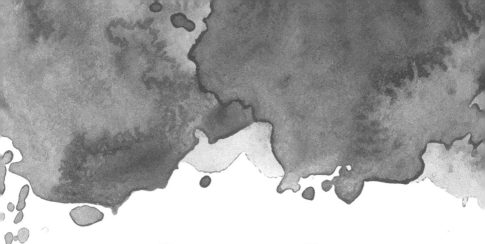

Chapter 8

INNOCENCE LOST

"Blessed is the one who perseveres under trial because, having stood the test, that person will receive the crown of life that the Lord has promised to those who love him." James 1:12

THE MAN'S VOICE gruffly asking, "Are you wearing knickers?" took her by surprise and brought her right back to the present. She was utterly shocked. Stunned! Did he really ask her that stupid question? Indignantly she responded "Yes," still so shocked that he would even ask her such an intimate question. What a stupid question for a grown man to ask. Why would she not be wearing underwear, she thought huffily.

He walked toward her, using a placating tone of voice, trying to give her a false sense of security. "We have to take off all our clothes and dry them by the fireplace. Let's go over there and we can warm up together."

She was shocked out of her innocent wits. She never undressed in front of any boys or men. In fact, she never undressed in front of anyone except her mummy or the servant lady when they had to give her a bath. What was wrong with this man? Her young mind knew instinctively that this was not going to go well. Placating voice or not, she knew instinctively that whatever it was he was planning to do, it was not going to be good or for her benefit. In fact, she knew it was going to be really, really bad. She looked around again frantically for an escape. Even if she could open that giant door, she didn't know which way to run. She felt like she was in the "Jack and the Beanstalk" story, and he was the giant coming to get her.

The decision to run had barely formed in her brain when it was quickly and decisively squashed. He grabbed her and pushed her toward the fireplace and said, "Let's get these wet clothes off you," in a stern voice, and attempted to unbutton her blouse.

She immediately felt a jolt of revulsion shiver down her spine, though at the time she didn't understand that feeling or the sickness that came over her and made her want to vomit. The tiny hairs on the back of her neck and back rose up to a standing position, sending cold shivers down her spine and through her body, a clear sign of danger. The blood in her veins chilled to freezing and she felt goose bumps tingling all over her skin. Panic, the size of an elephant, set in and she was spurred into action. She grabbed the front of her blouse with both hands tightly and refused to let him unbutton it. She shoved his hands away each time he tried again. She had a funny feeling in her body she couldn't describe, but it was sending her brain signals that this man's touch was not welcome and it was not right. She knew intuitively this was a sin. What he was about to do was a sin.

The more aggressive he got, the more terrified she became of some unknown calamity about to befall her. At first, she fought silently and angrily, violently pushing his hands away, willing him to stop touching her. Silence soon turned to soundless screams as he persisted in trying to rip her clothes off, handling her little body roughly, trying to hold her still with one hand while tugging at her clothes with the other. She sucked in large amounts of air, but no sound could be formed in her throat and mouth. But, even without words, she continued to fight him and surprised him and herself with the strength and fierce resistance she met him with. She used her hands, feet, and teeth to hit, scratch, kick, and bite him. He had no idea what wild animal he had conjured up from hell, but the ball of fierce energy and the thrashing cyclone of arms and legs that attacked him was definitely not what he had anticipated or bargained for.

Fear is the greatest motivator to get a little child moving or resisting violently the force she faced. She had no idea how long and how hard she fought to keep his hands off her, but alas, she was fighting a losing battle against his superior strength and brute force. He was overpowering her and there was nothing she could do about it.

After what seemed like an eternity to her, miraculously, she found her voice. She screamed and screamed and screamed. She felt such a sense of release at the sound of her own voice, she kept screaming even louder. No words could be formulated still because fear and terror had taken over her mind, her throat, and her voice at the thought of what he was doing to her. She couldn't quite understand or comprehend it all. She just knew in the pit of her stomach that it was horribly bad. He was a very bad man! He was a wicked man and he would go to hell for this. At the thought of hell, she became even more afraid, if that was even possible. What if he was the devil himself? He looked as ugly and as scary as the devil pictures she had seen before and only the devil would do what he was doing. The thought that he could be the devil galvanized her into a more desperate scramble for her life, and she screamed at the top of her lungs with that new fear. No words, no pleas, just terrified, shrill screams.

He tried to shut her up, to stop her screams by grabbing her face and covering her mouth. He pressed her cheeks between his fingers and thumb, squeezing tightly while he picked her up with his other hand and carried her toward the bed. Her inner cheeks caught painfully between her teeth as she tasted her own blood in her mouth. She struggled all the more furiously, kicking him and thrashing her arms around, grunting like a wild animal caught in a trap. She felt trapped. She was trapped, floating off the ground in the crook of his arm. She felt light-headed. Darkness threatened to engulf her as he dumped her on the bed and grabbed at her underwear and tried to pull it off her, but she bent her knees to prevent him from taking it off.

She felt the bed sink down as he threw himself down, half on top of her and half on the bed, grabbing her thrashing arms and holding them above her head while trapping her legs under him with his lower body. She became a wild animal then, throwing her head from side to side, biting him hard wherever her mouth landed, screaming in between deep, gulping breaths. He was not ready for such a violent assault from the little girl he thought he could overpower. She morphed from that little girl into a cornered, wild and ferocious animal, snarling and clawing at him. Her eyes felt like they could pop out of her head at any minute. Her throat hurt and her mouth felt dry. She felt her head was exploding into a million brilliant firecrackers, bursting in color and shapes, like the star lights she and her siblings were allowed to play with on the rare occasion.

Earlier that day, in her pure innocence, she thought that the worst fear was him taking her away from familiar surroundings. She had no idea until his attack on her little body what fear really was, and the evil that really existed in the world. This was a rude awakening and she was still innocent and unaware yet of what his intent translated to in actions. She just knew it was a horrible, horrible thing.

His body was so heavy on top of her and she felt her strength weakening in the power of his arms and his chest that were crushing her, but somehow, she found her own strength to keep fighting him. The bites from her sharp young teeth didn't go unnoticed by him as he yelped and tried to dodge her. Time had no meaning to her. Everything was either moving in slow motion or stood still in her mind. She started to lose steam, her energy waned and she cried weakly for him to stop it, that he was hurting her.

She kept saying, "It's paining, it's paining," but he was oblivious to her pain, or he chose not to hear her. She didn't know she was close to fainting. She may have passed out or gone blank a couple times as she fought him.

When she opened her eyes and saw his face barely an inch from hers, the look in his eyes terrified her. They were bulging and bloodshot red and she saw the reflection of the terrified child looking back at her. She didn't know what was more frightening, his eyes, or the girl looking back at her in the reflection: wild, frantic eyes, hair a mess, tear-streaked cheeks, quivering chin. She instinctively knew she had to look away, break eye contact, or be doomed and lost forever. He was the devil! Sharp pain pierced her temples like a knife was being jabbed into her head. She ground her teeth together as she shoved hard at him to dislodge him and it made her so weak. Her mind kept screaming, *He's the devil, he's the devil!*

She had no idea how long she struggled. She started to lose consciousness and in some odd way, she felt that someone had reached in through the top of her head and lifted her body out of her skin. She was no longer connected to the scene playing out in front of her eyes. Instead, she was watching it all happen in slow motion from some safe place in the distance. She saw her arms and legs move like a spider, in every direction, twisting and turning. She knew she was going to vomit all over him a second before it happened. She watched it happen in slow motion, as if she was in a dream, as projectile vomit spewed all over his face and chest. She saw his arm lift high in the air and come down and strike her face with such brutal force that her head jerked to the side and she stopped moving. But it didn't deter his single-minded pursuit of his objective. He was like a mad man who couldn't control his actions.

From her vantage point somewhere in the distance, in her mind's trancelike state, she looked like a tiny little bird fighting a gigantic hawk. She didn't stand a chance. How could she? All her spunk was totally useless against his brutal strength. She had passed out.

Years later, she would remember her valiant and violent efforts in trying to fight him off, and wonder where she got the strength and the courage. She remembered her resistance to his invasion of her innocence, but she didn't remember the physical and emotional damage he submitted her to that night. It was kept from her memory for decades only by the grace of God, to protect her mind from total destruction.

If only she had learned about the David and Goliath story in the Bible earlier in her life, maybe she would have come up with some intelligent way to defeat the monster of a man with whom she had the great misfortune of crossing paths.

CHAPTER 9

KNOCK ON THE DOOR

"But the Lord is faithful, and He will strengthen you and protect you from the evil one." 2 Thessalonians 3:3

MIRACLE OF MIRACLES, through her haziness and faintness, a loud pounding on the room door began to infiltrate her brain. Constant pounding, pounding, pounding, not letting up. *Thump-thump-thump*, followed by a man yelling angrily through the closed door in another language. She didn't understand a word he was saying. It was not English. She could not move. She could not find her voice. She could not think. She could not feel. She thought she was dead as she lay motionless under his weight. Why was he not moving?

She wanted to scream at him, "Get off me you filthy pig," but the words would not formulate and pass through her lips.

The commotion at the door finally penetrated the Visitor's brain. It took a few minutes or maybe seconds for the sounds to register. She watched him in a trance as he went very still on top of her body. He was breathless, as if he had been running. Then he frantically jumped off her, hastily pulling on his clothes and adjusting them, pushing trembling hands through his wet hair to settle it down. He was in full-blown panic. His fear was so visible on his face she could almost breathe it. He was truly afraid of whomever was on the other side of that door. Why was he afraid? She was the one who should be afraid, after what he just did to her.

Like a madman, he looked around him frantically for some means of escape from the banging on the door. Just like she discovered earlier, there was no escaping from this room, except through the front door. He was trapped here just like she was. He looked back at her, and leaning forward, he hauled her off the bed roughly. He dropped her on her feet on the floor. Searching blindly with his hand on the floor, he finally found her knickers and pulled them up her legs with jerking, trembling hands. He straightened her clothes with quick, jerky movements.

Finally, with a gruff command, he choked out words that sounded like, "Don't make a sound or I will belt you," before he hurried to answer the door.

Her confused mind registered him opening the door and speaking to the man on the other side. He held the door half-open/half-closed as he conversed with the man outside, attempting to sound reasonable and calm, all the while not allowing him a glimpse into the room. The man must have been the hotel proprietor or manager. Perhaps another guest had heard the screaming of the young girl and contacted reception or the concierge desk with concerns for the child, or simply because they were being disturbed.

As she stood there near the giant bed, she felt her knees knocking against one another, and to her shame she felt hot, wet liquid roll down her legs to form a puddle on the floor. She had just made a vee-vee again for the second time that day and the shame of it crushed her. In that moment, her bodily reaction to her circumstances was more damning and shameful than anything else she could imagine. She was supposed to be a big girl and know when she needed to use the toilet. Utterly defeated, she rubbed her hands over her clothes as if to make sure that her body was covered. Her trembling legs couldn't hold her body upright and she slid to the floor, weak and numb with fear, and another feeling she couldn't identify. Sobbing silently, she put her face in her hands, and sliding her feet toward her bottom, she brought her trembling hands and face down to her knees. She couldn't stop the trembling as she sat curled over her knees and cried quietly until she had no more tears.

After a long, drawn-out, angry conversation, maybe an exchange of money, or reassurance that all was well, the hotel manager retreated and faded into the corridor behind him. She wanted to yell out to him to stop, to come back immediately, not to leave her alone with this monster, but the words got stuck in her throat. She couldn't speak. She couldn't feel her legs, she couldn't move to run after him. She wanted to yell at him to come back and help her to get away, to tell him what this man had done to her, but she didn't know what words to use to explain it. She didn't know, she didn't know. She couldn't understand any of it. And, it terrified her to even think about it. Why did he do this to her? Why? How was she going to tell her parents about this? Were they going to be angry with her?

All thoughts of going to sleep on that bed had vanished. In fact, that bed no longer appealed to her because that was where this wicked man had done the most wicked thing to her. She trembled uncontrollably and tried to wipe away those images from her mind. She wished he would leave the room. She wanted to run away and hide from him. She wished God would punish him and he would burn in hell forever. He deserved to burn in hell. Maybe the devil would scare him when he went to hell. She hoped he would be in hell forever and ever.

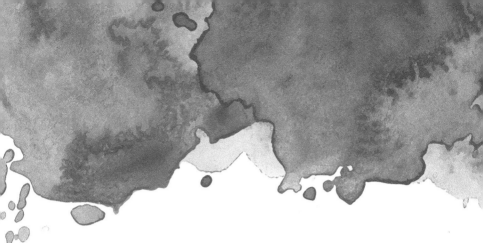

Chapter 10

THE MELTDOWN

"For I know the plans I have for you," declares the Lord, "plans to prosper you and not to harm you, plans to give you hope and a future." Jeremiah 29:11

SHE HEARD THE Visitor shut the room door and lock it again. With fear and dread running through her veins, she looked up through her fingers to see him turn and walk toward her. Her heart sank as she realized the man at the door had left her alone to face the Visitor and she was once again alone with her attacker in the locked hotel room. She felt abandoned and alone, left to face this monster of a man all over again. She tried to scoot away from him, but her limbs could not move.

She could tell her kidnapper was furious with her. No, he was stark raving mad. He reached her in a few strides, and grabbing her under her arms with both hands, he shook her vigorously, all the while screaming at her for drawing attention to the room. He told her she was a "stupid idiot" who had just ruined everything. He set her back down on her feet and slapped her so hard across her cheek that she fell to the floor with its force. His face was distorted and ugly and she had that fleeting feeling again that he was the devil himself. Terrified, she tried to scramble away from him on all fours. He came after her, snatched at her skirt and pulled her backwards into a kneeling position. Leaning over, he seized the front of her blouse and lifted her in the air and snarled words at her that she could no longer decipher. Her brain didn't want to function anymore.

He dumped her back on the floor and advanced to the bed, where he sat down and dropped his head in his hands, gulping for air like a severely wounded animal. He hit one tightly closed fist into the palm of his other hand over and over again, shouting more obscene words into the air. He stood up and paced back and forth muttering to himself like the madman she thought he was, shaking his head vigorously. He looked like a stray, mad dog on the street, frothing from the mouth, snarling at anyone or anything which got within striking distance of him. She was so scared. She could feel her heart pounding in her chest so loud and fast. She felt the trembling begin in her chest and move to her arms, shoulders and feet. She shook visibly. She was in a full-blown case of the shudders with no way of being able to control it. She couldn't understand why her daddy hadn't found her yet. How she wished her he was here now to protect her from this monster.

She was terrified by his outburst and the anger she sensed in him. She bit her lip and tried to remain silent for fear of provoking another bout of violence against her. She remembered the scary ghost stories her uncles narrated when they were minding her and her sisters. They told them of black magic being done to people to cast the evil spirit on them. She didn't like to hear ghost stories because they scared her so much and she couldn't fall asleep at night. The images the ghost stories conjured up would haunt her at night and she would wake up terrified. Maybe, she thought, someone had done some black magic on him and the evil spirit had entered his body? Yes, that had to be it, she was sure of it. That was why he had turned from a friendly stranger into this monster.

Finally, after what seemed like a lifetime, he stood up resolutely. His mind was made up about something. He angrily told her they had to leave immediately. He could barely keep his fury at her in check as he started to put his shoes back on. He was mad at her because it was her fault they had to leave and go back out in the pouring rain, when they could have enjoyed the dry, warm, and cozy hotel room.

Her young, innocent mind didn't register that she had been granted a reprieve by the hotel manager. She didn't know at that time that the angry man in front of her in that hotel room had damaged her mentally, emotionally and physically, and she would never be able to speak of this incident to anyone for years and years.

She didn't even realize that some unknown entity had miraculously intervened and saved her life. Would he have killed her after he was done with her? Or, had things worked out for him at the hotel, would he have kept her as his unwilling companion until he got tired of her and moved on to the next victim? Only he knew, and of course, God knew.

Many years later, she realized God gave her strength in her weakness because she was His child, and He was her Protector and Savior. Only because of His grace and mercy was she saved from being killed in the hotel room or at some point later. The Visitor could have killer her and disappeared into the monsoons, and no one would have known better.

God, in His infinite wisdom, also allowed her to bury the memory of that unspeakable experience so deep in her subconscious that it would take her decades of building emotional and mental strength to face those demons again. All she remembered was his name, but she would never utter it in her lifetime, if she could help it. She would toss it into the deep shadows of her subconscious, where she compelled it to remain together with the dreadful events of that day.

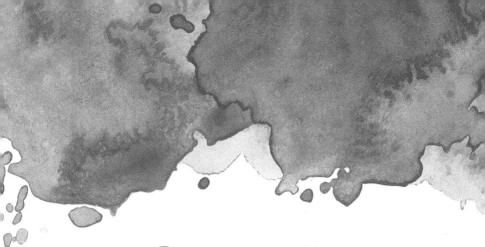

CHAPTER 11

FAILURE TO PROTECT

Forgiving is not a hard thing.
It is trusting again that is most difficult.

DECADES LATER, SHE would come to understand that the man at the door was probably the proprietor or hotel manager who didn't want to have any part of what was going on in that room. She would question why that manager allowed the man to leave the hotel, taking her along with him, instead of alerting the authorities or protecting her by taking her away from the situation she was in. Instead, he allowed the man to leave the hotel with a child who was so obviously traumatized and afraid of him, if her screams were anything to go by, allowing him to disappear into the darkness of the monsoon rains. Did he not care about what would happen to her? Surely, he knew the man was up to no good with a minor child in a hotel room, and a screaming one at that. If he couldn't summon up sufficient compassion as a father, could he not have done so as human being and aided a helpless little child?

Did his conscience allow him to sleep at night, not knowing whether any harm had come to the child? Did he have any children of his own? Did he know what he had interrupted at that time? Did he feel any pangs of guilt or ask God for forgiveness for not doing the right thing? Did he wonder, after they left the hotel, if she had been murdered and discarded somewhere, to be swept away by the torrential downpour?

She tried to make excuses for him. Maybe he thought the man was her father, and the girl was probably just tired, cold and cranky. Maybe he thought it best not to interfere with a family man. And then again, maybe the Visitor bribed him with money, not an uncommon thing in India, to keep him from contacting the police.

Getting back to the hotel manager, she couldn't give him the benefit of the doubt because she knew in those days and in that culture, the "man" was in charge and women and children didn't have a voice. He would not have had consideration for the child if the Visitor informed him that he was her father or uncle. At the end of the day, she was just a child, no reason to lose sleep over her. She was of no consequence. She could have been a stray dog he wanted the Visitor to get out of the hotel immediately before the guests found out, for all the attention he gave her. It was better to get rid of both of them, the man and the child, so the hotel's reputation would stay intact. Neither she nor the Visitor were his problem anymore. Good riddance to bad rubbish, as the Anglo-Indians would say.

They left the hotel the same way they entered it, through the back door, not encountering anyone on their way out, not a guest or an employee. Except for the reality of what he did to her and what he took from her, it would almost seem the whole episode didn't happen. The hotel manager never laid eyes on her, so it was almost as if she didn't exist except for the complaints about a screaming child from a hotel guest or two.

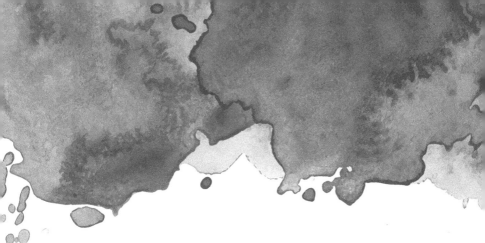

CHAPTER 12

ABANDONED
BUT NOT ALONE

"The Lord Himself goes before you and will be with you, He will never leave you nor forsake you. Do not be afraid, do not be discouraged." Deuteronomy 31:8

AS SOON AS he pushed open the hotel's exit door, they were hit by the pouring, drenching rain again. Back on the bicycle again. Back to riding "doubles" on the crossbar with her captor, the madman. He was mad. Madder than a rabid dog in the street. His anger was beyond words. He couldn't speak except for grunting loudly and angrily while he kept smacking her on her head with his open palm, and hitting her back and shoulders with the ball of his fist. He kept cursing her, using words she had never heard in her young life, for making such a racket and drawing attention to the room and to him. She should have felt pain from the blows, but she was so caught up in the aftershock of his violent attack on her little body and her senses in that room, the pain didn't register at the time.

It didn't even register she had fought so valiantly and violently during his assault on her. A tiny little girl fighting off a military man instinctively, with energy and strength she didn't know she possessed, which seemed to have come from nowhere. The survivor in her, even as a little child, somehow was able to understand that she had to fight if she wanted to get out of this situation and get back home to her family.

On and on they rode, well into the night. She didn't know what he was thinking, what he was planning, where he was taking her next. She was so exhausted physically and mentally, she didn't even entertain the thought that her ordeal was not over yet, or maybe it was her innocence and unworldly naivety which made her believe he was taking her back home.

She would start to doze off and he would angrily shove her slumping body back to a more upright position. How rude of him! She had long since lost track of time and place. The only light was the little Dynamo lantern attached to the handlebar of the bicycle, which did very little to break through the darkness. He seemed to know his way around though, and kept cycling on through the rain and deeper into the seemingly unending night.

After what appeared to be a lifetime, he stopped the bike near an abandoned ramshackle building, got off it and pulled her off it too. He propped the bike up against the broken wall and told her to wait with the bike. He said he saw two military policemen following him earlier and he was going to hide for a little while until they went away. He peered into her face and told her he would come back to get her and take her back home once he got rid of the military police. She truly believed him, because she wanted so badly to go home. He left her there and disappeared into the night. Forever.

She didn't realize at first that he had no intention of coming back for her. He had no plans to take her back home. He had given up on her. She was too much trouble. Maybe he was afraid that since the hotel manager had seen him with the child, the police were on the lookout for him. Later, she realized he was looking out for himself and his only thought was to get as far away from her as possible. He left her there, all alone. Her captor had abandoned her. He left a tiny little girl-child exposed to the elements and whatever other potential danger she would face in some unknown place, far away from home. Left her to face certain death from hunger, exposure, and emotional and mental terror.

How long she waited beside the bicycle at that wall for his return was anyone's guess. The only light in that dark world was the dim yellow light from the Dynamo on the front of the bike, but it started to flicker and she knew it would die soon. She moved slowly from one foot to the other in the dark to warm up her stiff legs. She felt like a statute made of ice. She hugged herself by wrapping her thin arms around her body and leaned against the wall for support. She didn't feel hunger pangs anymore. She was long past hunger. She didn't expect to see anyone or any movement because it was so dark. She didn't even think about going home anymore. Her mind was numb. Her body was tight with pain. She was really and truly alone in this place. She was abandoned. No one would be able to find her because they didn't know where she was. She didn't know where she was. She slid to the ground and rested her head back against the wall. Her brain was starting to shut down or was close to dead.

Men's Bicycle

She may have dozed off while leaning against the wall, but survival instinct cannot be ignored, even as a child. She kept startling awake every few minutes. Had she stopped breathing? Did her heart stop and start back up with a jerk each time? Was she dead? She couldn't tell. She couldn't even feel it when she pinched herself, because her skin and flesh were numb from the cold. Why didn't she just give up? She could have just slumped down to the ground near the bike and allowed her aching body to give in to the desperate need for sleep. The rain water would have risen over the hours and drowned her for sure.

Still in an upright position against the wall she may have settled into a dream of some kind or was dwelling in limbo, a safe place in her mind. She woke up with a jolt, as if something or someone had just called her name, quite loudly. In fact, she was very sure she heard her name resounding loud and clear in her brain. Whoever it was, whatever it was, it was meant to get her moving again so she wouldn't die there that night from hours and hours of exposure. She realized the awful man was never coming back to get her. He had lied to her. She was alone in this unknown, dark, and God-forsaken world.

She had no inkling of what gave her the strength to pull herself up to a standing position and to put one foot in front of the other, to move forward. She had no idea what to do or in which direction to go. But she must go. She marshalled up all the energy she could and started to walk, away from the dilapidated building, away from the broken wall that was propping her up, away from the bike on which she had gotten to this lost location. She just simply moved forward into the darkness as if she was being led by the hand, into the unknown world in front of her, with no idea which direction was home. She walked on blindly. Little did she know that she was, at the tender age of six, walking by faith and not by sight, literally.

As she walked heedlessly into the night and into the black, unwelcoming world, away from the flickering light of the Dynamo, her thoughts wandered back to her family. What were they doing now? The thought of her parents worrying about her made her cry. She wailed out loud, but she knew no one could hear her, even if she screamed. She didn't know how to describe the way she felt, but years into the future she would relive those feelings of sadness, disheartenment, and defeat. Her heart was as heavy as stone in her chest. Yet, though it made her sad, she sought asylum in the warmth of memories of her family and her home.

The rains continued, relentlessly beating down on her battered and fragile young body. How much could one little child endure? Apparently, quite a lot. She would learn soon enough that in her weakness, God would give strength.

She felt compelled by some unknown force to keep walking, her thoughts in a whirl as she flitted from one memory to another of her siblings, her parents, her neighborhood friends. She pictured her daddy coming home from work on his bicycle, propping it up against the wall in the compound, shutting off the lantern on the handlebar, taking his lunch bag off it and entering the house to sit down at the heavily scarred wooden kitchen table. She pictured him running his tired hands through his hair and rubbing his forehead as if to relieve pain. And she could hear her mummy saying, "One of you children, help your daddy to get his shoes and socks off," while she placed his dinner in front of him. She envisioned herself and the other siblings sitting around and waiting for him to finish eating his dinner, because he always left the last or last few mouthfuls of rice and curry on his plate for whichever of the children were at the table with him.. He would tell them that God's blessings were in those last mouthfuls, and he made sure to feed each child one of those last mouthfuls to make sure they each received God's blessings. Sometimes, if food was scant, the siblings would have to take turns each evening during the week to get that last mouthful of blessings.

Eating that last mouthful from her father's hand, even though she'd already had her dinner earlier in the evening, always made her feel especially happy and content. The children had no idea how their parents managed to feed them and take care of them. The children were unaware of the sacrifices they made to ensure they were always taken care of. Later in life, when she had a better understanding of their status in life, she promised herself that she would pay them back in every way she could for all the sacrifices they made, so their lives would be comfortable.

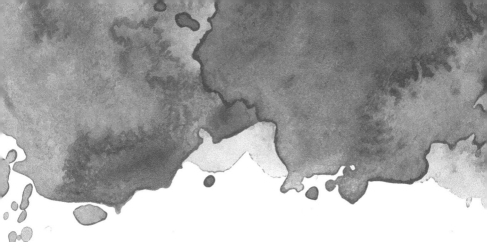

CHAPTER 13

FAMILY LIFE IN A BRITISH COLONY TOWN

Family is the cornerstone of a community.

HER MATERNAL GREAT-GRANDFATHER was an Irish gentleman who owned a horse-and-carriage business in India. He and his wife were killed in an accident on one of their carriage trips, rendering her young teenage grandmother an orphan. The young girl was sent to live with her three spinster aunts, who did not have the wherewithal or the experience to take care of a teenage girl. As family lore had it, when the aunts learned that an Anglo-Indian gentleman had just arrived from Burma (now called Myanmar), in search of a bride, they immediately set about meeting him to offer the fifteen-year-old's hand in marriage. Post haste, the aunts set about arranging a marriage with this thirty-something gentleman and the bashful, innocent, teenage girl. She bore him eight sons and two daughters. Family reflection reveals that he treated her like a queen.

Her paternal grandparents were British-Indians who also settled in the south of India in a British colony town. They raised three boys, and two girls. The two girls died in infancy. Her parents met, fell in love, married young, and had a large family. They were typical Anglo-Indians. Her parents dressed and behaved more British than Indian, not unlike many of their neighbors and friends in the town. They were a jovial bunch of people and loved to entertain. Friends and neighbors often dropped by in the evenings and they would play guitars, makeshift drums and instruments they creatively put together hastily in the compound, and they would dance until late into the night.

She thought her mummy looked so lovely when she got dressed up in her calf-length dresses, gathered at the waist, with imitation pearl necklace and earrings, matching purse and shoes. She had beautiful curly, silky hair, which she wore quite short. Her daddy looked so handsome with his curly black hair and long sideburns that reached down to his chin. She loved to watch them dance together in the compound with the other neighborhood couples and friends. She imagined herself trotting around on high heels and looking as graceful and beautiful as her mummy.

The children were not allowed to mingle with the adults, but occasionally, one of them would sneak out into the compound to grab a snack or two, or to cause some mischief or the other before disappearing back into the house. For the most part, they had their own fun and games indoors to keep them entertained and busy.

With their excellent command of the spoken English language and their ability to read and write in English, the British engaged Anglo-Indian men to work in prestigious jobs on the railroads, at post offices and various business offices, banks and factories. Her great-grandfather on her father's side and her grandfather on her mother's side held leadership positions in the gold and coal mines.

Anglo-Indian women were homemakers for the most part, or if they worked, they were hired on as secretaries. They were outstanding cooks and excellent dancers who could jive, fox-trot, waltz and jitterbug like any Western woman when they attended the various balls and dances at the many British-Indian clubs. They raised their children, managed the budget, and made sure their husbands were happy and content. The Anglo-Indian meals were a mouth-watering, finger-licking, tears-in-your-eyes, delicious combination of English dishes fused with Indian spices and herbs.

Indian Powdered Spices

Indian Whole Spices / Herbs

Indian Meal

Indian Meal Platter

Her daddy was a hardworking man and the only earning member of the family. Her mother was a homemaker and took care of all the children and some of their cousins. Though they were poor and struggled to make ends meet, her parents were generous to a fault. They never turned anyone away. Their home was always open to family, friends, and neighbors. Her home was a place where people came for a cup of coffee or tea, maybe a bite of something to eat, for advice or conversation, and on occasion, for a place to lay their heads for a night or two. Her home was a popular gathering place.

Even though they didn't have much, the children learned to share everything they had with whomever stopped by to visit or to seek help. Her oldest sister once shared a story about their father reprimanding her for complaining about having to share the small amount of food they had with visitors who showed up at supper time. He reproached her with, "Don't ever say that again, we must always share everything we have." The children learned generosity and hospitality at a very early age. They were happy kids who enjoyed the simple pleasures of life. They were content with what little they had because they didn't know any better. They were secure in their parents' love.

Her father got paid once a month. Payday was a big deal for the children because he would come home with special snacks for them and they would line up to receive their pocket money from him, a quarter of an Indian Rupee. He turned over his paycheck to her mother, who managed the household and somehow made the money stretch for the month. Her parents made innumerable sacrifices to ensure the wellbeing of the entire family. Her father frequently worked long hours, putting in overtime at the factory to supplement his salary to provide for their needs. He was always pleasant and the perfect gentleman, even when he was afflicted with exhaustion. Yet, the hard times were always good naturedly dismissed with, "God will provide."

Indian Currency

Years later, she was touched and filled with sadness and immense pride when she read his journals. He began each month with a page dedicated to a prayer to God, outlining his earnings and his family expenses (which always seemed to exceed his salary), requesting God humbly to please provide for all of their needs.

Once a year, usually on December 1, when their father got his annual bonus, he and her mother would take the children on a bus ride to the market, something the children looked forward to with great anticipation and excitement for weeks and weeks. The bus was a large diesel vehicle that labored noisily along the narrow streets, filled with a mix of clean, well-dressed passengers as well as filthy, smelly, barefooted passengers packed into every bit of floor space like sardines. If all the bus seats were taken, the standing passengers hung on for dear life as the bus took the bends in the road too widely or too tightly. And one had to pity those poor passengers hanging on to the window bars or on the platform steps in the front and rear ends of the bus, who barely had a foothold or any support to keep their balance.

Her parents had quite a chore trying to keep track of all the kids as they got on and off the bus. And they had to watch them like eagles, for stray hands of wicked men who would try to sneak a pinch or cop a feel of a young girl's bottom. The combined smell of diesel fumes, spices, smoking and chewing tobacco, cigars, snuff, and betel nut[1] permeated the crowded bus, filled her nostrils, and often made her feel extremely nauseated and sick to her stomach. But she and the other children gladly accepted any discomfort and were willing to make any sacrifice just to experience the sheer joy and pleasure of this much-anticipated family outing. It was the most joyous event for this little girl.

The first stop was the tailor shop, where each child got to choose their own material and a pattern for an outfit from the tailor man's old and tattered "fashion" magazines. He would take their measurements and send them off with a promise to have their new outfits ready before Christmas. The family would walk to the shoe stores on another street from the tailor's as the children chatted excitedly about their new clothes. They moved from store to store until each child found the pair of shoes they liked and their parents could afford. This was such a special family event because they didn't get new clothes and shoes throughout the year, except for Christmas. Otherwise, almost all of their clothes were hand-me-downs or were given to them from other family members or friends.

Finally, the most anticipated event of the evening, a meal at a local restaurant where they would be ushered into a "family" room for privacy. The children were allowed to give the waiter their food selection, followed by an after-dinner cup of the famous hot, creamy, and frothy coffee. Yes, even as children, they loved the specialty coffee. What a treat and what an adventure, to be discussed for days to come while waiting in excited anticipation for their new clothes for Christmas. Their joy and pride overflowed when they would dress up in their new clothes and shoes and go to church for late evening or midnight service on Christmas Eve.

On Christmas morning, their mummy would make a special Christmas breakfast the whole family would demolish, after which the children dressed in their new clothes again, made their rounds to the family and friends' homes in their town to wish them a "Merry Christmas," and partake of the delicious snacks they were offered. At each home they would be served special "Christmas trash," as they called it; specifically, rose-cookies, khul-khuls (deep fried treat made with flour, semolina and sugar), fruit cake or plum cake, and usually a little sip of home-made Christmas wine. By the time they returned home, their tummies would be stuffed with goodies and they would be ready for a nice, long, happy and dream-filled nap. They didn't usually get Christmas gifts, mostly because they couldn't afford such luxuries.

She was very young when she was sent to a British boarding school (convent) with several of her sisters. Their parents did not have the funds to pay boarding school fees, but they were fortunate to have connected with their father's high school teacher, a European gentlelady, who made her home in India. She took great interest in the children, determined to encourage them in every aspect of their lives. She involved them in choir practices at her home and had them participating in the choir at Mass on Sundays, at weddings and special events. She encouraged the children to enter singing competitions and accompanied them on the piano. Her home became their second home, where they were treated to all sorts of special treats and entertainment. She was determined to assist their parents in providing them an excellent British education. Using her influence, she enrolled them in a British convent (boarding school), situated on top of a hill over the plains of Salem, Madras State (now renamed Chennai), located on the Bay of Bengal in Eastern India. The journey by bus from their hometown to Salem, Madras, took a solid eight hours or more. It was an additional two-hour bus trip from the plains of Salem up to the hill station where the boarding school was located. This involved a harrowing bus ride, traveling along the deadly Ghat System (road system engineered/constructed during the British Raj period), which provided access routes connecting the "hill stations" in the mountainous ranges of the Indian subcontinent to the plains below.

Allowing their daughters to become boarders at the convent was the best decision her parents made for them. Even though they were poor and couldn't afford the school fees, none of the other students were aware they were given free education through the influence of their father's high school teacher. They were treated like any other well-positioned family who sent their children from as far away as England, Bahrain, Kuwait, and other foreign countries and islands. She enjoyed boarding life, once she got over her initial loneliness and homesickness. The structured, sheltered life with the nuns was exactly what she needed to forget her traumatic ordeal and to thrive once again.

Anglo-Indians were socialites and cherished their evening get-togethers with good conversation, dancing, singing, a game of cards, Housie (Bingo), or a board game of Caroms. The children enjoyed good times playing in the compound or on the pavement in front of their home. There was a constant stream of neighbors, friends, and visitors stopping by her home; some stayed for the evening while others stayed overnight. There was always a kettle whistling on the stove and her parents shared whatever little rations they had with everyone who visited. Her father was not only soft-spoken and a perfect gentleman, but kind and generous. Her mother was the homemaker and disciplinarian. She spanked them for whatever mischief they got into and warned, "Wait till your father gets home." The children giggled, knowing he would take them into the other room and pretend to spank them by hitting the bed, while they yelped as if they were being beaten. They believed their mother was fooled, but she knew what was going on all the while. Of course, their father never spared the rod when they deserved it.

They were loving and caring parents who struggled financially, but they always put their children first. Though they couldn't give their children fine earthly treasures or riches, they gave them an unforgettable childhood and a Christian education. They taught them to share everything they had, to be generous to a fault, to be kind and compassionate, to look out for the underdog, and drove home the point that simple things in life brought more joy and happiness than all the riches in the world. It was an easy, relaxed, simple, and open communal way of living. Everyone was happy and content.

Home from boarding school for the holidays, she and her siblings looked forward to going to the many dances at the British-style clubs. There was always a chaperon in tow, usually an older uncle, much to their dismay, who kept a watchful eye on them. There was a "dance" to celebrate every event: Christmas, New Year's, Valentine's, May Queen, June Rose, Independence Day, Guy Fawkes Day, and so on. They looked back and laughed at the embarrassment and mortification of having their uncle show up on the dance floor, at the stroke of midnight, to pull them away from their dancing partners because it was "time to go home."

Then there was Amateur Night at the "Club," when her father and his friends, and she and her siblings competed in singing the latest songs they'd heard on the BBC (British Broadcasting Corporation) or VOA (Voice of America) radio stations. They taught themselves to play the guitar and were thrilled to win first or second place in their age categories. Her father's idols were famous Anglo-Indian singers like Cliff Richards and Engelbert Humperdinck, who made it big on the Hit Parade and other radio and music venues abroad. He loved Jim Reeves and Elvis Presley.

Whenever her parents could get away for an hour or two to visit with friends or for a card game, they had a long list of babysitters ready to assist. Her mother had lady friends drop in for a cup of tea or coffee during the afternoons and to discuss the latest romance book they had read from "Mills and Boon." One of the neighbor ladies who loved to read the daily newspaper would often stop by to share or discuss the latest scandal she'd read. At a very early age, the girl learned all about the "Watergate Scandal" in America, and later about the attempts to tumble Skylab into the Indian Ocean, through the renditions of this newspaper-reading neighbor lady. Of course, the children were taught to be respectful to their elders and were not allowed to participate in adult conversation, but that didn't stop them from eavesdropping on their conversations. They had their ways.

Living in India wasn't easy, especially for the poor-to-middle-class. Struggling to make ends meet, her parents found new and ingenious ways to stretch her father's monthly pay through the end of the month. Sometimes when they were low on rations, her mother would feed all of the children out of one community pot to ensure that all of them had something to eat, even if it was just a couple bites. The girl loved it when her mother fed them by hand. They would sit in a circle around her and would carry on a spirited conversation, blissfully unaware that their mother was counting every piece of meat and every piece of potato so she could divide them up equally among them.

Her parents wanted desperately to give their children an opportunity to make better lives for themselves in another country. They attempted to immigrate to Australia when she was very young, but were rejected. The Australian Consulate General reckoned just one working member in the family wouldn't earn sufficiently to raise such a large family. They were devastated by the rejection and no one could have been more disappointed than her father. Luckily, all was not lost. Nine years after the Australian rejection, she immigrated to the USA as a young adult, and paved the way for her parents and the rest of the family to follow.

Corruption was commonplace in India and nothing was accomplished without some form of "baksheesh" (bribe). Nothing ever happened without money passing under the table. She experienced the unmitigated corruption herself when she was immigrating to the USA and needed a copy of her birth certificate. Her father accompanied her to the municipal office to obtain a copy of the certificate. They arrived at the office at 8 am and were instructed to sit on a bench on the veranda to wait until someone could meet with them. Individuals would come out to update them on progress and suggest that they go out for a "coffee." Her father was expected to not only foot the bill but to pay a bribe the man demanded. They returned to the veranda and waited for another hour or so until a different individual gave them another update and suggested going for "lunch." This went on until 4 pm, when they indicated the certificate was ready. However, they didn't hand it over until they extracted more money from her father. But alas, cunningly, they had prepared the certificate in the local Indian language, which they knew the US Embassy would not accept, so her father had to bribe yet another individual to redo the certificate in English for the American Consulate.

It broke her heart and angered her that they manipulated and extricated refreshments, lunch, and money from her father that he could barely afford. He worked excruciatingly long hours to earn a reasonably decent salary, of which every paise (penny) was accounted for. She promised herself that once she was settled in the USA and was allowed to sponsor her family, she would do everything in her power to help them to immigrate to a better life.

She kept that promise by sponsoring her father first, as soon as she became a US citizen (five years after her initial entry into the USA as a permanent resident), and the rest of the family followed according to plan. She kept, among her souvenirs, letters from her father expressing his joy and happiness at the prospect of traveling to the US Embassy in Madras for his immigration interview and medicals, and his excitement and thankfulness that finally, his dreams of immigrating and making better lives for his children were about to be fulfilled.

She will always treasure the fact she was able to make her father's dream possible and give him the opportunity to live and work in the USA as a proud American citizen. The joy it brought him to successfully bring the entire family to America, to give them the opportunity to make better lives for themselves and their families, was beyond compare for him. After the Australian Embassy's rejection, when he thought there was no way, God made a way. No man could have been prouder than her father to be selected to serve on the jury in his local county. It was one of the most joyful highlights of his life.

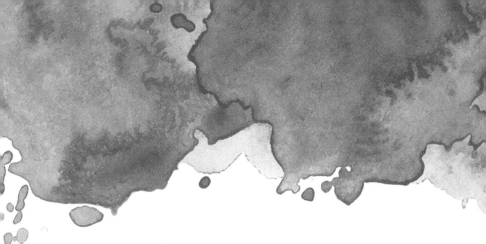

Chapter 14

A VISION, A MIRAGE, OR HER IMAGINATION

"God is our refuge and strength, an ever-present help in trouble. Therefore we will not fear, though the earth give way, and the mountains fall into the heart of the sea." Psalm 46:1-2

HER MIND RETURNED to the present, still wandering through the unknow terrain in the non-stop pouring rain, exhausted beyond conscious thought, no idea where she was heading or where she would end up. Her eyes were open, but she couldn't see beyond her outstretched hands. She had no idea how long she'd been out there in the wilderness, feeling like she was in a foreign world, another time zone. Not that she really had any concept of time other than morning, evening and night. But gradually, like the unfolding of a slow-motion dream, she realized there was a smudge blurring her vision, or was it in front of her somewhere in the distance? She rubbed her wet face and eyes and peered into the distance, and that smudge still remained. Uncertain whether the smudge was in her eye or whether it was external, she wondered if she was going blind. She kept her focus on the smudge and continued walking toward it. After a while, she concluded the smudge was looking bigger, so she quickened her pace, walking as fast as her tired legs could carry her. She was not imagining it. The smudge became a spot of yellow. She tried to keep her eyes open against the rain because she was afraid to lose sight of the light. It drew her closer and closer like a welcoming beacon on this stormy, rain-saturated night.

After what seemed an eternity, she saw stick figures below the light, and after more walking, with strained and burning eyes, she could see those stick figures were actually people. Before long she heard the buzz of conversation. The closer she got, the more detail she was able to determine. These were men in traditional Indian clothing, not like the men in her family who dressed in British slacks and shirts. These men were dressed in Lungi[2] with Banyans.[3] They were standing at a Kaka[4] shop. The window had a tin awning under which the men crowded to shelter from the rain.

Lungi, Traditional Indian Men's Clothing

She couldn't believe her eyes. She had not seen any living creature, human or animal, in hours, and here she was looking at a group of village men in nowhere-land, smelling coffee and tobacco smoke. She experienced a feeling of giddiness mingled with hope and fear. Was she dreaming? Was this a vision? Was her mind playing tricks on her? Would this scene in front of her dissipate if she took a step forward? She had no idea how long she stood there on the outskirts of the little group, uncertain of what to do, but after what seemed like an eternity, the decision was taken from her when one of the men turned around and spotted her. Was he surprised to see her? He carefully walked toward her as if afraid he would scare her away. She was obviously not one of the villagers since she was not dressed like one of them (she was dressed in an Anglo-Indian skirt and button-up blouse).

When he reached her, he motioned for her to step under the tin awning and then proceeded to pour coffee out of his cup into the saucer and handed it to her. She drank it thirstily from the saucer, remembering her daddy doing exactly the same thing when he was drinking coffee and she wanted some. He had to be a good person, just like her daddy. He paid the shop keeper for a banana. She watched in fascination as the shop owner cut a banana off a huge hanging bunch in the corner of the window. The man handed her the banana, which she ate hungrily, enjoying the sweetness and texture on her tastebuds. She had been a very long time without food and she relished every morsel. If she could have stomached the banana skin, she would have devoured it too. The man continued talking to her softly in his language even though he knew she didn't understand a word. Her heart skipped a beat when she heard him mention the word "bus," because she knew that word. It meant there was some form of transportation even in this far-away place.

Seeing her reaction to the word "bus," he immediately motioned for her to follow him, opened a large black umbrella, and stepped away from the Kaka shop. She obediently followed him along the mud road, which was literally a pathway of mud and slush, totally forgetting that she should not go anywhere with strangers. She followed close on his heels, afraid to lose sight of him in the rain. He was her lifeline to her home. Soon they came upon a makeshift little bus shelter, barely visible through the wall of rain pouring down. There was a concrete slab for a floor and palm tree leaves and branches woven together, which made up the roof and one wall. He sat down on his haunches, and cupping his hands together, lit a match stick. Holding the lit match with one hand, he pointed to the numbers roughly written or scratched in with charcoal on the floor with the other hand. She was just learning her alphabet and numbers, but she easily recognized the number "19," which she was very familiar with. It was a number she had saved to memory since she often had to catch the Number 19 bus to go places with her family. She knew the Number 19 would take her back to her own town. She excitedly pointed to it. He seemed to understand and sat down on the floor, Buddha-style, and pulled her down to sit beside him. It was still dark and it was still raining. She shivered as she settled in to wait beside him. It seemed like an eternity of silence passed between them, but it was an easy, comfortable silence. She didn't feel threatened, she didn't feel afraid around him. She just sat in a silent daze. Maybe subconsciously she realized she was safe, that she might be finally on her way back home to the love and safety of her family.

She started to dose off next to her rescuer and automatically started to recite her night prayer in her mind, which her great-grandmother and her mummy often recited with her siblings and her.

Angel of God
My Guardian Dear,
To whom God's love
Commits me here,
Ever this day,
Be at my side,
To light and guard,
To rule and guide. Amen.

Many years later, she would think about her ordeal and the little night prayer she learned from the time she could speak. Perhaps God had sent her guardian angel to her in human form to bring her home? Or was it the Holy Spirit who guided her and there was no real human sitting beside her? Maybe it was a magical dream that God spun for her so her confused and tired mind could endure the ordeal?

Guardian Angel

It amazed her to think that even after that fateful day and night of living through the worst hell any child could experience, she continued to grow and thrive from that innocent child into the well-adjusted woman she became. She believed only through the grace of God was it possible for her not to surrender to the elements and give up, because He was not ready to give up on her. He had a plan for her life.

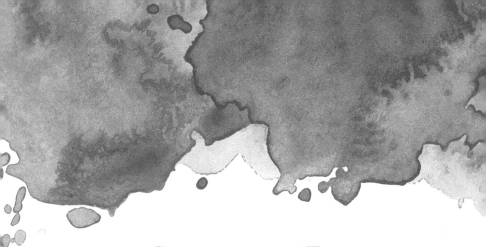

Chapter 15

THE JOYFUL REUNION

God is in control. He works all things for the good of His people.
Romans 8:28

EVENTUALLY, AFTER WHAT seemed an eternity, the Number 19 bus pulled into the bus stop and the man climbed on the bus with her. She absentmindedly noticed there was no conductor on the bus to collect the ticket money from them. She and the man who befriended here were the only passengers. Even though it was very early in the morning, she knew the bus should be crowded. Why weren't there any other people on the bus, she wondered. She stared at the empty seats and thought it was strange, because the buses were never empty. In fact, people were always crowded in like sardines, standing in the center, clinging to the hand straps on the bars above their heads, trying to keep their balance, shoving and pushing their way to a more secure position.

Every time she looked toward the front of the bus, she noticed the bus driver casting quick glances at her with something akin to pity in his eyes. She lowered her eyes and went back to her dreaming, the images of crowded buses still on her mind. Exhaustion took over as she felt the now familiar aching in every bone and muscle in her body. She knew she would not be able to move again as weariness drained her of all energy. As consciousness slowly slipped from her mind, her senses dulled and she slumped against the man beside her and dozed off into a restless, disturbed sleep for a little while.

She couldn't recall how long she slept, but she was awakened with a start when the bus rode over a bump in the road, jerking her already hurting small body into awareness of pain. She looked around in confusion at first, but then scenes outside the bus window slowly registered in her brain. She noticed it was slowing getting light outside and she started to recognize streets, buildings, landmarks. Excitement and a feeling of pure joy filtered into her brain and it warmed her blood, spreading through her veins, into her body, until it reached her extremities. She was coming home!

Hope and excitement mingled together and started to deliver energy and life back into her limp body, her heart and her mind. She was coming closer and closer to home. Her heart was pumping so fast she had to press her hands to her chest to prevent it from popping right out. She caught her breath and began to gulp in mouthfuls of air. Her excitement was palpable. This was definitely not a dream. This was real. She was in her hometown.

As the bus turned the bend onto the main street, she was amazed to see the lights were on everywhere, the street was filled with cycles, scooters, and people. She recognized people from her town. She didn't realize at the time, but people in her town, friends and neighbors of her family had been out searching for her all evening and all night, traveling through the town and the nearby towns. She had no awareness of how scared and worried her parents, her family and the town's people were for her safety. They all thought she would not return home alive. The hours had turned into panic and fear of the worst outcome. They never thought they would see her again.

No one was really paying attention to the bus as it turned on the main street and made its way to the bus shelter in front of her home. They were not expecting her to ride in on a bus. The man got off the bus first and she followed him on trembling legs. She couldn't speak for the pure emotional joy and relief as she recognized the faces of her family members. Exhaustion took over her senses as she stood at the bottom of the bus steps, waiting for someone to notice her. She had no words and she had no voice. The scene in front of her, with bright light streaming from the lamp posts and brightly lit homes, reminded her of postcards and Christmas cards showing a busy Main Street with so much activity. It felt like a dream, but she knew instinctively it was not. The sights in front of her would forever be etched in her memory. It gave her a warm, tingly, lovely feeling.

Finally, someone spotted her and exclaimed, "Oh my God, there she is, she's home, she just got off the bus!" and everyone started crowding around her, all talking at the same time in loud voices, grabbing her, hugging her, saying, "What, child, what happened to you?" She heard someone, maybe one of her uncles, say, "Where is that bugger? I'll break his legs for him," but using harsher words that she was not allowed to use. She knew he was asking about that monster of a man who kidnapped her, but she couldn't find any words to speak as she was swept up in the crowd of people as they moved toward the open gate of her home. Her uncles and the townspeople would not hesitate to beat him up if he showed up in town again, but for now they were so glad to have her back home where she belonged. She was safe, thank God.

The state of her wet, dirty, and torn clothes was explained away by the drenching rains and the gusty winds she had walked through. Her swollen face, red eyes, weakened physical state, and bare feet would also be put down to the rains, exposure to the elements, and starvation. As the women steered her into the house to bathe her, dry her hair, change her clothes and feed her, she turned to look back at the bus and the man who had brought her back home. She imagined she saw the man pat her father on the shoulder as she caught a glimpse of him before he disappeared back on the bus. Were those tears she saw in her daddy's eyes as he bowed his head as if in prayer? She couldn't tell, but at this point, she could no longer differentiate between reality and dream as her tired mind and body sought the comfort of her bed. She was so happy to be back home with her family. She felt safe and secure again in their love and happiness to see her and hug her. After a much-needed hot bath, some delicious comfort food, and a change of clothes, she finally gave in, curled up on her parents' bed, and fell into exhausted sleep.

She didn't know how long she slept, but when she woke up, she knew her parents were ecstatically happy to have her back home and were grateful that she suffered no apparent lasting physical or mental damage that they were aware of. They showered attention on her, gave her whatever she asked for, and amid tears and conversations they got the information they were looking for. She had been taken by the Visitor, and after hours of cycling around, he dropped her off in some town far away. She walked and walked in the rain until she found the man who brought her back home.

Nobody asked her about what the man did to her while they were gone. Whether to avoid agitating her or to protect her from such memories, she didn't know. Maybe her parents had warned everyone against bringing up the subject, for fear of triggering some mental trauma. Times were hard and her parents did the best they could to raise and protect their children. They relied on family and friends to watch out for them. They were always in need of free babysitting services, which the extended family provided when one or two of the children had to be taken to the hospital for some childhood ailment or the other. It was especially necessary to have a backup child-minding plan during those times when the children were hit with childhood diseases like measles, mumps, chicken pox, whooping cough, etc., and they succumbed one after another.

Now, after all they had been through over the past twenty-four hours or more, they relied on the family to rally around her like never before, to help her forget the entire ordeal and to get back to the daily routine. Nobody really wanted to delve deeper, into her recent memory, probably because they didn't want to hear what they feared they might hear from her.

In India, any kind of therapy was out of the question, especially in that day and age. Counseling or therapy for sexual assault or sexual abuse, let alone kidnapping, was not something they could expect. They lived in a time and place where women and children had no voice, so going to the police would have done absolutely nothing unless there was an exchange of money under the table, which her parents could not afford. Even if they could afford it, any kind of therapy would have had a negative connotation and she would have been considered a mental case, something her parents and family would shield her from.

Instead, her parents believed the best therapy was to get her back into the daily routine of family life with her siblings and other family members. They figured life would get back to normal eventually, except that the adults would be more watchful of strangers or anyone outside the family in the future.

Fear and doubt had worn her out. For years she blamed herself for what happened to her. She believed she deserved to be punished because she disobeyed her parents and went off with a stranger, exactly what they'd instructed the children never to do. But in spite of her disobedience, she knew her parents loved her, and they would have gladly given their lives to have saved her any pain.

Looking back on her experience all those years ago, she realized she could never have survived the ordeal through her own strength alone. The supernatural strength of the Living God saw her through and brought her home to her loving family. She knew God loved her, and when she thought there was no way out of the situation she was in, though she was unaware of it at the time, He made a way for her. She came to realize that fact later on in her adult life and she grew to believe strongly and unerringly in a merciful and loving God who was compassionate and forgiving.

As she grew in maturity, she realized there was nothing more important in life than God and nothing more binding than family. She came to believe and rely on the following important truths. God shapes you, not from birth, but in your mother's womb. He loves, protects, defends, embraces and shelters you in the good times and in the bad times. He gives your life purpose. And nothing binds more compellingly, powerfully, and lovingly than family and she belonged in such a family. Experience showed her that family will stand by you when you need them, forgetting all prior offenses and hurts, letting their protective natures and deeply anchored love engulf and cover you like a soft, warm, velvety blanket.

CHAPTER 16

BACK TO THE ROUTINE

SHE REGRETTED THAT she was never able to or never given the opportunity to talk about that ordeal with her parents or any of the elders during her childhood. As a result of having no professional support to get her through the days and weeks after her traumatic experience, the fear, guilt, and shame drove those unbearable memories into hiding. She felt she was in chains, held captive by some unseen force, unable to open up to anyone. She felt trapped. Though she agonized over it and felt such intense unrest in her soul, she could not bring herself to put into words the secret she had locked away. She felt that once the words were vocalized, she couldn't take them back and hide them away. She was certain as soon as everyone knew her secret, they would despise her. She couldn't quite explain why she blamed herself for years, other than the remorse and shame she felt for being disobedient. She reasoned with herself that the blame was hers because she took that ride on the bicycle with that man in disobedience, therefore God had punished her.

No one raised the subject again during her formative years or offered her comfort. In the days that followed, she would wake up from bad dreams and nightmares of being trapped. She had one recurring nightmare she couldn't shake off for years. She dreamed of being in the park behind her home. Dusk would be falling, and still, for some stubborn reason she would linger, knowing her parents would not be happy with her for disobeying them and staying out after dark. Then, when it got too dark to see, she would hurriedly try to get to one of the park exits to leave, but when she reached the top of the stairs to exit between the stone pillars, there would be tons of snakes curling around them, hanging down from the trellis, and preventing her from leaving. Terrified, she would turn and run down the stairs, screaming at the top of her lungs. She would turn around and run to another exit where she would be met with the same nightmare scenario of dangling snakes preventing her from leaving. She continued to run from exit to exit until she was exhausted and found no way to escape them. Eventually she would wake up from the nightmare in a sweat, in a weakened and fearful state, her heart pounding erratically, afraid to go back to sleep, afraid to even close her eyes. She would stare at the roof, willing herself to not shut her eyes. Every sound, every slight movement would intrude on her senses and cause her to remain rigid with fear.

Gradually she got back into a routine and she learned to conceal her nightmares and fears from everyone. The images of that monster's face in her young, impressionable mind remained extremely vivid through the years; not his features, but the distorted ugliness of his expressions and raw emotions. They would be conjured up time and again in her nightmares and terrorize her. Some days and nights were better than others, but invariably, something or someone would trigger that fear. The fear and anger stayed with her. She could not allow her painful feelings to surface and she would not share those feelings with anyone because of her fear that she would be considered weak. It took countless years of practice for her to perfect the art of losing herself in that quiet place in her mind she had created to retreat to. Her parents assumed she was daydreaming, but she knew it was safe in her sanctuary, where the nightmares and fears could subside for a short time but were never alleviated.

CHAPTER 17

SOUL SEARCHING

EVENTUALLY SHE WOULD be sent to boarding school with several of her sisters. The structured and religious life the nuns administered helped her to blot out the awful experience from her mind for the rest of her childhood. She remembered on one occasion when her catechism teacher, a nun, told the story of Jesus dying on the cross for everyone's sins, she desperately wanted to confess her sin of disobedience. She was sure the nun would understand since she cried for Jesus when she told the students His story, but at the last minute she could not articulate her confession, and let the opportunity slip away. She wouldn't dare tell the priest during "confession." He scared her half to death. He was a huge man with a booming voice and he was well known for yelling at the girls in the confessional. She was terrified that he would speak her sin out loud when he instructed her on the penance she must perform as atonement for her sins, and his loud voice would announce her sins throughout the hushed silence of the chapel.

Though she never found the courage or the words to talk with the nuns about her ordeal, she would forever be grateful for the lifeline that boarding school offered. Attending early morning Mass every day, benediction on Wednesday evenings, Sunday services, being given the coveted responsibility of reading the Epistles on certain days during Mass, being immersed in the Easter retreat (taking a vow of silence and reading only religious literature during those three days of retreat), and the routine ritual of praying kept her focused and trusting in God. In time, she was able to get past her brokenness through self-analysis and soul searching. Finding the root cause for her fear, she realized she was not to blame for what happened to her. She could not have controlled the circumstances or the actions of the evil man who came to visit. He was the devil personified.

After she immigrated to the USA, some of her siblings who remembered that fateful time, and recalled how terrified they felt at the thought of her being lost forever, would occasionally bring up the subject and ask questions. However, she had become reasonably skilled at hiding her emotions. She had locked most of those memories away and would only discuss what she was comfortable speaking about, specifically, the monsoon rains, the darkness, and the hotel manager banging on the door. She could even tell them about the Visitor asking her if she was wearing knickers, but not anything more than that. She wasn't sure what she was more afraid of, not being believed, being judged, or just plain afraid of reliving undesirable memories. So, she chose to let them believe the man was stopped from doing the "nasty" by the arrival of the hotel manager at the door.

Yet, certain things would trigger her memory, and fear would immediately take possession of her mind. She would be walking on a deserted street or waiting at a bus stop, and if she saw a man walking toward her, she would immediately, as subtly as she could, cross to the opposite side. She was afraid he would attack her. If she got on an elevator and there was just one man on it, she would pretend she forgot something and get off immediately. She was afraid he might trap her in there, alone with him. She never allowed any strangers to come into her home and she never opened the door to anyone who knocked unless she could identify them as family or friend. If she had to go to a new place, or a job interview, her husband would have to drive with her the evening before to familiarize herself with landmarks so she wouldn't get lost. Most people didn't understand her fear, but she did. The fear of being lost or trapped and the terror associated with it continued to plague her for countless years. She was terrified of getting lost.

Did her mind create this marvelous fighting fiend of a child who fought the visitor with all the fierceness of a banshee, until the hotel manager showed up at the door? Or was she just a terrified child who froze when he attacked her and had his way with her? Her mind never let her travel that far into her subconscious for the answers. Suffice it to say, she was better off not remembering. Or, maybe God considered it best to blot that memory out completely and gave her different memories to keep her from losing her sanity. Maybe, it was best locked away in the deepest recesses of her mind, never to be exposed or re-lived until the time was right.

She would ask herself questions over the years, and the only answers she could come up with were the same rational responses, which encouraged her to believe it was God's way of putting her mind at ease after the horrendous torment she had been through. She needed to trust in order to accept.

Was the little shop in the middle of nowhere and the man who saved her in the middle of a monsoon real? Or did it all happen in her imagination to keep her from losing her mind and succumbing to the perils she faced? Was it the Holy Spirit in the form of the man who stepped away from the imaginary shop and imaginary crowd? Was it the Holy Spirit guiding her, leading her out of the wilderness and setting her back on the right track to a bus stop and the Number 19 bus that would carry her tired, aching body back to her family and hometown community?

"Why would there be a Kaka shop in the middle of nowhere?" There was no explanation for it to be open during the downpouring torrential rains and gusting monsoon winds. The only answer she found to be most reasonable was the Kaka shop was a familiar experience for her, so therefore would put her at ease right away. There was a Kaka shop across the street from her home, which her parents allowed her to walk to and purchase small items.

"Why did the shop keeper sell bidis, coffee and bananas?" The answer seemed logical to her. These items were familiar to her. She often was sent on an errand by one of her uncles to purchase a banana or a packet of bidis. The smell of bidis would immediately put her at ease, since her uncles smoked them all the time. As for the bananas, she loved them. She loved to eat them rolled in a slice of bread or in a chapati (Indian flatbread). It was her comfort food.

"Why did a strange man offer her hot coffee in a saucer to drink?" There was no reason for any sensible person to be out in that weather standing in the rain, drinking coffee at a tiny window in a makeshift shop, with the wind bellowing all around him. Yet, the smell of coffee and its heat as she sipped it were meant to comfort and put her at ease, because it was something her father always did. She would not be frightened by the stranger because his kind gesture reminded her of her father.

If the Kaka shop, bidis, banana, and coffee were not real, then the only explanation she would accept therefore was that the stranger was a supernatural being sent by God to guide her to safety, in answer to her prayers.

The constant barrage of questions that plagued her during her young adult life would abate for a period of time while she focused on raising her son (her miracle baby God favored her with), and being the best mother in the world to him. She protected him with the fierceness of a mother lioness.

She knew what the enemy meant for evil, God used for good in her life. She believed the God she trusted would not let her be outwitted by the devil. Satan, with all of his cunning, was no match for her because she was a child of the Almighty God.

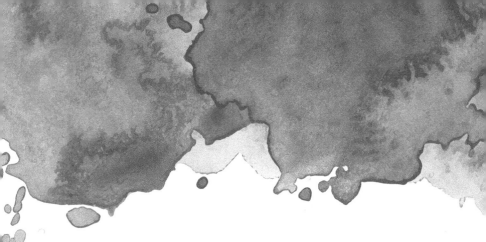

CHAPTER 18

HER GUARDIAN ANGEL OR THE HOLY SPIRIT

"To trust God in the light is nothing, but trust Him in the dark – that is faith."[5] *– Charles Spurgeon (English Baptist Preacher)*

SHE GREW INTO a young, independent woman and experienced many trials, tribulations, and miracles. She resisted thinking about her ordeal through those years, until her son was about four or five years of age, and she watched a video with him about a little boy who fell down a dry well. The little boy was confident that his father would find him and save him, but as it got later in the evening, he began to lose hope and yelled out, "Help, I am all alone." He heard those words echo back down into the well, "all alone, all alone, all alone," and he became terrified. But Jesus spoke to him in the silence of the well, echoing the words, "You are not alone, not alone, not alone." Her son wanted to hear the reassurance that God was always with him and that he could speak with Him at any time. He loved to watch that video over and over again with her. For her, it was a reminder of the time when she reached out to God in all her innocence and aloneness, and He not only answered her prayers but walked with her all the way to safety.

The video took her back to that time when she was lost in the monsoons. As memories slowly permeated her mind, she started to relive the events surrounding that horrible time and realized she had escaped death. As an adult, she had no doubt her kidnapper would have killed her had the circumstances been right for him. Or, having escaped her kidnapper, she could have died in the torrential rains, flooding, muck and filth that the flood waters held. She was so exhausted from hunger and exposure to the elements, she could have lost her footing and fallen in the calf-high water. As exhausted and bone-weary as she was, she wouldn't have had the energy or strength to pick herself back up and would have drowned. So many potential scenarios and possible outcomes. How blessed she was to have come through that horrendous ordeal.

If he was real, she would never know the name of the man who saved her and brought her back home. She would never get the chance to thank him. She would never know whether he was real, a figment of her imagination, or her guardian angel. Maybe even the Holy Spirit? In her mind, she had the vivid recollection of him handing her the saucer of hot coffee and the banana. To this day, she could smell the delicious aroma of the coffee and feel its warmth as she sipped it. That might explain why she cannot drink coffee unless it is piping hot. She can still picture in her mind's eye the two of them sitting on the concrete slab of the bus shelter in peaceful and comfortable silence, while they waited for the bus, and the long ride home with him seated next to her. She can feel the strength of his shoulder as she laid her head against it and fell asleep. Yet, somewhere in the back of her mind, there was a lingering doubt whether he was human or angel. Either way, she would never forget him. She considered him her guardian angel.

She knew as an adult what she didn't know as that innocent little child. The attack was real, her reactions were real, her fierce resistance to the visitor's physical demands on her body was real. She realized in her adulthood that she was not successful in fighting him off and keeping him from his obvious intent.

Likewise, she had no doubt in her mind that there was a supernatural force that saved her life. It kept her from harm all those years ago in the lonely and cold world of water and darkness and continued to bring her through challenging events in her life to this day. She believed God heard her repeated prayers and sent the Holy Spirit to be with her. He gave her a helper to free her from her burdens of fear and physical weakness.

She was safe and comfortable in the presence of the man at the bus shelter and on the bus taking her back home. In the power of those moments, she was too little to know what she was living through or experiencing, what was dream or reality, what was human or supernatural. She experiences those same feelings of safety and comfort to this day when she seeks the Lord with all her heart and soul. She feels His presence in the darkest times of her life, which gives her the peace she needs to survive whatever she is going through. She has learned to lean on Him for guidance and strength.

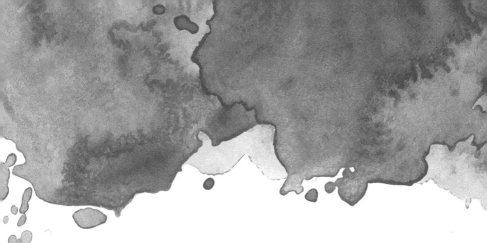

CHAPTER 19

THE POWER OF PRAYER AND PERSEVERANCE

"I can do all things through Christ who strengthens me." Philippians 4:13 (NKJV)

No matter what you face, be confident that God will not waste your pain. He sees you in your wilderness and enfolds you in his mighty, protective arms. The power of His presence will encourage you and carry you through your pain. All you need to do is call on His name and believe that He hears you and He will arm you well for any battle you may face.

ALL HER PREMONITIONS, her instincts and insights over the years have made her realize her belief and trust in God have seen her through the very worst in her life. He is always there when she needs Him. He is faithful! If you seek His presence, He will show up. Your life can be transformed by putting your faith in Him. How true it is: seek Him and He will show up!

Now, as a woman and a mother, she knows that every-thing happens for a reason and God will never leave her or forsake her. He is the answer in every situation. He is bigger than any problem she faces. **He will make a way where there is no way.** He will open the door that she needs to walk through. All that is required is to bring everything to Him in prayer and He will fight the battles.

She learned to always have faith and depend on His mercy and grace. She learned to never give up because He always keeps His promises. He is always just a prayer away. She realizes now that every problem or hurdle she faced in life were in reality gifts from God, preparing her for some-thing bigger in her life. Her strength and courage to face situations head-on are examples of those gifts. She believes that everything happens for a reason because God's pur-pose must be fulfilled. Looking back now on when the Lord found her all those years ago, hopeless and helpless, she knows she was never alone. He was, and still is, just a next breath away. She takes her strength and courage from her own experience of God's faithfulness. Her trust in God is well-founded and secure.

How could it be any other way when God pulled her through that traumatic experience and redeemed all that was broken in her life? He would not let that ordeal lead her to a dead end. Instead, He opened her mind, her heart, her life to a truth that there was a God who wanted to give her a life of abundance. She knew her story was a story of divine mercy because God saved her from a watery grave out there in the monsoon wilderness. She held on to hope, that word she didn't have in her vocabulary at six years of age, even when she was out of hope. She didn't know what the word *miracle* meant either, but the fact that she walked away from her kidnapper, survived the deadly monsoon rains, and found her way back home after hours of exposure to the elements was indeed a miracle. She has learned not to give up hope in any situation, no matter how difficult and how hopeless it may seem.

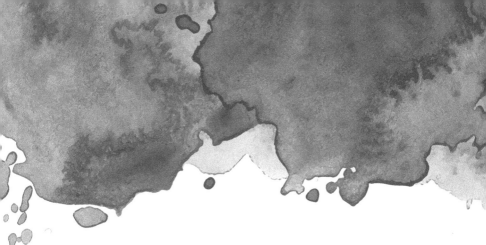

CHAPTER 20

EPILOGUE

"We are hard pressed on every side, but not crushed; perplexed, but not in despair; persecuted, but not abandoned; struck down, but not destroyed." 2 Corinthians 4:8-9

WHAT DID IT take to make her reveal her deepest secret to the world all these years later? The secret she shoved to the darkest recesses of her mind, never to be revisited? What made her break her tight grip on that tamperproof lock that secured the gates of her memory?

She had sworn she would never go back to the terror of that time, yet certain events persuaded her to write this book. The emergence of the "Me Too" movement, which revealed the courage and strength of the women who opened up their deepest wounds to support each other, to be heard and believed, convinced her it was time to face her own fears.

The "Me Too" movement helped women discover they are not alone in their fears. Their voices must be heard and what they have to say is not just important to reveal the perpetrators of sexual abuse, but also to help those who are afraid to acknowledge they were victims.

The author hopes her readers will be inspired by her story and find peace and comfort in leaning on God. As a mother of a miracle baby and as a breast cancer survivor, her faith in God was strengthened by her experiences. She believes God uses people as vessels to help others live through their trials. She strives to be the person God uses to bring peace and comfort to others.

After her son was born, the fierce, obsessive protectiveness she felt for him compelled her to dig deeper into her memory, to allow brief glimpses of forbidden memories. Those glimpses made her extremely protective with her only child. She promised herself no one would ever get close enough to him to harm him. She never let him go into a men's bathroom by himself. If her husband was not able to accompany him, she would stand at the door with her foot propping it ajar while her son was inside. She would call his name every few minutes, and if he didn't respond she would march right into the men's room to check on him. Not a single man who walked into that bathroom ever asked her to step aside or to shut that door. She watched over her son like a hawk.

Children especially are afraid to come forward because they don't think they will be believed. Most of the time they don't even understand what happened to them and therefore do not know how to express themselves. They blame themselves, believing they deserve what happened to them because of something they did or didn't do.

Parents and guardians of little children must always be aware of the dangers lurking around in plain sight. These precious little ones depend on their parents and guardians for protection. Be wary of anyone and everyone, even people you know, including your family and friends. You may believe they have the best intentions, but when it comes to your children, you must be extra vigilant. Perpetrators are often relatives or family friends, which makes it even more difficult for a child because the family trusts them. All it takes is a few minutes to lose a child. Her advice to everyone is, "Watch over the children God entrusted to you like hawks."

Teach children about inappropriate touching; teach them what is allowed and not allowed by strangers, family members or friends. Imbed in their minds that any touching is inappropriate, even if someone offers to just change their clothes. Children must learn from an early age that only certain people are allowed to wash and bathe them, change their clothes, etc. And, most importantly, let them know they must tell their parents or elders if someone does try to touch them or show them inappropriate material.

If a child shows signs of fear and wariness around certain people or indicates he/she has been sexually assaulted or abused, please believe them. Most importantly, get them the therapy they need to help them cope with the situation, rather than let them suppress their pain. A child will heal physically, but without help, the child cannot heal emotionally. Not having the opportunity to talk about the trauma is devastating to a child. It only intensifies their pain and prolongs their suffering. Given the opportunity to confront their fear, children can find proper healing. And don't forget to pray in all situations and have faith in God, always.

One afternoon shortly after she informed her siblings about writing this book, she had an opportunity to spend an entire afternoon with several of her sisters. She was amazed at how the fact that she had written about her traumatic experience opened up the floodgates and they were able to frankly and honestly converse about events they had never shared before in their own lives. She appreciated that this conversation was long overdue, and it proved to be healing and cathartic for all of them.

For this writer, the darkness in the wilderness was like an enemy who shows up at the least expected times, trying to convince you to give up. The enemy wanted to destroy her that day. But God had other plans for her life. Somehow, even at the tender age of six, she knew she couldn't stop and she couldn't give up. If she did, it would have been the end of her. She needed God's supernatural powers to overcome the power of the evil one. God was stronger than any force, and her only source of help when she was helpless, vulnerable and exposed to all the dangerous elements. Oh, but the enemy had no idea how stubborn she was, what a fighter she was! God made her brave so she could walk through that dark world of torrential rain without fear, oblivious to the dangers all around her. She was single-minded in her intent to find her way back home to her family.

Though she didn't know it then, her faith was born that day in the midst of the legendary monsoon rains, the darkness and the sinful, evil intentions of one man. It would be strengthened with each challenging event she faced in the future. In her weakness, He gave her strength.

In conclusion, don't let what is going on in this world consume you. Instead, focus on His Word and the plans He has for you.

The End

ABOUT THE AUTHOR

LORRAINE THERESA AUSTIN was born into a large family and raised in South India, where she survived many a daunting experience. She was the first in her family to immigrate to the USA as a young adult, paving the way for the rest of her family to follow and share in the American Dream. She faced incredible challenges and hardships but did not let them hinder her. Sheer determination to succeed and excel in her career took her from the lowest rung on the workforce ladder to a successful and reputable position within a large organization, establishing and cherishing close relationships and lasting friendships along the way.

She fancied sharing her life experiences with people in the form of short stories. Her desire to help people overcome their struggles with situations through her own life experiences prompted her to write this, her first book.

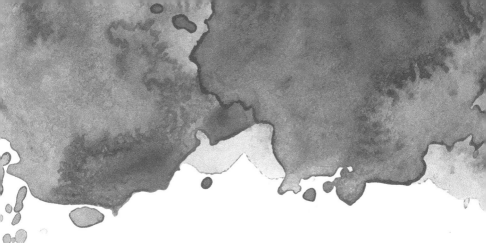

ENDNOTES

1   Betel nut is also known as areca nut, which is a chewing concoction of betel nut and betel leaf called Supari in the Hindi language.

2   A long length of material wrapped around the waist

3   Sleeveless undershirts for men

4   A tiny, makeshift shop with just a window through which the owner sold coffee, bananas, and bidis (rolled tobacco leaf)

5   Charles Spurgeon, *The Complete Works of C. H. Spurgeon, Volume 13: Sermons 728 to 787.* (Delmarva Publications, 2015), 91.

CPSIA information can be obtained
at www.ICGtesting.com
Printed in the USA
BVHW062254290321
603635BV00013B/838

9 781662 810329